Breaking Bread
— and —
Drinking Martinis

(Tales of Sharing
and
Sharing of Tales)

BY PETER F. LANGROCK

ONION
RIVER

PRESS

Burlington, Vermont

Onion River Press
89 Church Street
Burlington, VT 05401
info@onionriverpress.com
www.onionriverpress.com

ISBN: 978-1-966607-24-3

Library of Congress Control Number: 2025912533

To my grandson, Peter Anthony Camardo, who challenged
me to write this book.

Table of Contents

— Introduction —

Breaking bread is more than sharing food. It is sharing a sense of personhood and festive spirits and meaningful connections. It can be as simple as a wink from the person in the next seat when you are at a ballpark enjoying a hot dog with too much mustard. It can also be a formal state dinner with many toasts and speeches. However it occurs, it changes, at least in a small way, good or bad, your relationship with that person. This book concentrates on the positive side of breaking bread. Even sharing a cup of coffee with a witness at a deposition or a stranger standing in line waiting to vote changes your perspective and relationship with that person. I intend to share my experiences and the related tales that have given so much meaning to my life.

The "drinking of martinis" is a placeholder for the role alcohol has played in my life. To me, it is similar to the breaking of bread. I treasure many positive memories that have resulted from enjoying it—almost always with other people. I have chosen the phrase "drinking martinis" as the placeholder for all alcohol libations because martinis have most often been my drink of choice, leading to many happy occasions and related tales.

My grandson, Peter Camardo, graduated from Northeastern University in Boston in December of 2019. Northeastern has a co-op system where the academic year is set up as four quarters, two of which are in residence at the school and two are working experiences in the real world.

Peter majored in business, and during one of his co-ops, he worked for a financial firm. This firm offered him a job after graduation. Scheduled to begin July 1, 2020, Peter had a six-month gap time between graduation and starting his work career. He planned to take a trip during this gap with a buddy to Asia traveling by motorbike through Laos, Vietnam, Cambodia, and ending up in Taiwan. He was then planning to go to Milan to work as an au pair for two months to help an Italian family's children learn English. Then bang. Covid hit. He was in Taiwan when international travel began to be shut down. He decided he had better get back to the United States as soon as possible. There was no question of going to Milan, as Milan was the epicenter of Covid in Italy. He luckily got on one of the last planes leaving Taiwan for the United States before that travel route was banned. After arriving in Boston, he quarantined himself for fourteen days and then came to visit us.

What started as a short visit ended as a stay of five months. Due to Covid, the starting date of his job had been moved from July 1st to September 1st. The world was in a shutdown mode, but we made work for him on the farm. He was overqualified for the fence painting he was doing. Luckily for Peter, he got a call from his future employer who indicated they had a new contract and that they could use his help starting immediately and working remotely.

He lived with us, earning approximately what he would have earned had he been working full time in Boston but with the advantage of having no expenses. It gave him a chance to save a little and get a head start on the world of independent living.

The spring and summer of 2020 was pre-vaccination, and our world was governed by careful masking, social distancing, and working remotely. We spent most of our time at home, which resulted in an increased interest in planning, preparing, and experimenting with food. The pandemic caused many restaurants to close, and there was suddenly a surplus of oysters. Island Creek Oysters would ship 100 oysters via Federal Express for next-day delivery for as low as $85.00. In a period of ten weeks, we consumed 800 oysters. Peter became an expert shucker. We set a pattern of enjoying oysters on the half shell every evening with our cocktails.

At one of these cocktail hours, we began discussing some of the favorite meals I had had over the years. Peter asked how I could remember so many special meals. I told him I could probably recall 1,000 times I had shared a meal or drinks with family or friends. He challenged my assertion that I could recall so many happenings. Over the next several months, every day I would remember times of sharing, and those stories became fodder for this book.

The year of 1960 was a banner year for me. I finished law school, graduated, got married, ran for State's Attorney, got the nomination, passed the bar, got elected, got sworn in to the bar, and started practicing law. The job of States Attorney was a half-time position paying $2,000 plus $400 towards expenses. However, the other half of the time, I could develop a private practice.

In 1961, for the sum of $13,500, Joann and I purchased a 110-acre farm. In 1968, we bought an adjoining farm with 170 acres for $27,000. This is the house and farm where we still live. We have three successful children and six wonderful grandchildren.

While my law practice has never made me rich in dollar terms, it has provided me with enough money to educate my children, help my grandchildren, and allow us to travel throughout much of the world. I enjoy rural life, maintain a small farm, and hunt and fish at leisure. I feel very rich.

I looking back over my career, I have been involved in fascinating litigation in Vermont in many venues around the United States (and even outside the United States), including four trips to the United States Supreme Court. My interest in bar activities has brought me in contact with many significant people involved in our changing country. Looking back over this career, I realize that the most important memories are not the cases that I won or lost but the people I met. I have always been a people person and memories of my friends, colleagues, and clients give me the greatest pleasure. I also realize that almost all of those memories include breaking bread or sharing drinks.

With the challenge from my grandson, I decided to turn some of my experiences into this book. It is autobiographical in part, because I can only really write about what I know and have lived. Some of my experiences have resulted in good stories I want to share with you.

CHAPTER 1

Oysters

I have a love affair with a restaurant in New York: the famous oyster bar at Grand Central Station. I first came to the restaurant when I was a student at the University of Chicago in the 1950s. The Empire State Express, a train running from Chicago to New York, ended at Grand Central Station. After about sixteen hours of sitting in coach, finally viewing one of the most scenic stretches of any railway—the east side of the Hudson River south from Albany to New York—I was ready for something special. That something special was at a stand at the Grand Central Oyster Bar. The stand was equipped with heated cooking pans that tipped into a bowl from a swivel. Upon ordering, the cook, dressed in white, put a large spoon of butter, fresh shucked oysters, and some cream into the pan. He added Worcestershire sauce and paprika to make an oyster roast. As soon as the edges of the oysters started to curl, he flipped the content of his swivel pan into a waiting bowl, and it was instant heaven.

Over the years, for both lunch and dinner, I have dined there with many friends under its unique vaulted ceiling. There are two bars; one has a long white marble top stretched along the front wall just to the right of the main entrance. At the end of the bar closest to the entrance is a rack that contains twenty to thirty bushel baskets of oysters, each one harvested from different locations. Above the rack is a chalkboard with the names of the harvested area and the price for each oyster. Some names are familiar, and some are unknown. You would place an order asking for whatever number of oysters you wanted from any particular location. The waiter took your order and handed a slip to a man at the shucking station who would reach into the appropriate baskets then shuck the oysters and place them on a tray with shaved ice. They were then served to you with a slice of lemon, cocktail sauce, a vinegar sauce, and some oyster crackers. While you sat at the bar, you couldn't help being enchanted by the show of the shuckers at work. As I watched the shuckers and waited for the oysters to arrive, I would always have a martini.

Some people prefer white wine with their oysters, but martinis are my first choice. This decision led to an interesting encounter. I was sitting at the bar next to a man who had just finished a tray of twelve oysters. He called for the waiter as he had decided to order another dozen. When my oysters arrived, I was still drinking my martini. I "cheer" tipped my martini toward my neighbor and started on my oysters. I realized my companion at the next stool over was drinking white wine. I made a comment, and this started a discussion as to which was the best beverage to accompany oysters. We soon established that we agreed that oysters on the half shell are the supreme gastronomic experience but differed on martini vs. white wine. During the course of this discussion over oysters, we dissolved into a friendly relationship. We still have never resolved which libation is the more appropriate accompaniment. His name is Richard Dupuis and subsequent correspondence between us built a friendship that has resulted in several meetings in New York. His knowledge of oyster bars in New York far exceeds mine, and over the years we have met at several of his suggested venues. He has visited me in Vermont at our farm, and Joann and I have visited him and his wife Karen in Connecticut. Oysters were always present.

Richard is a financial advisor based in New York City, and my law practice is 250 miles to the north. Fortunately, my practice takes me frequently to New York, often for an argument before the United States Court of Appeals for the Second Circuit. That has allowed us to maintain our friendship over oysters and our preferred libations. When he visited our home in Vermont, he presented my wife with a lovely antique oyster dish—a flat dish with five indentations along the edges for placing the oysters. I had never seen this type of dish before, and I have since learned that they were once in common use and today are sought by collectors. In some of our meetings in New York, we invited lawyers who were joint counsel with me on the cases that brought me to New York—Terry Reed and Martin Gusy. Terry and I worked together for many years, and Martin I met at the VIS competition in Vienna.

Over the years, Terry and I had traveled together on cases from London to Tokyo. We adopted the custom of using the Welsh expression "lechyd da!" (to your health) rather than saying "cheers!" when we lifted a drink. I picked up this toast while drinking in a large number of pubs with a Welsh farmer, Alun Jones.

Martin was to be married in Westport, Connecticut, and both Terry and I were invited to the wedding. This was convenient for a reunion with Terry and our spouses and with another old friend, Richard Dupuis. The evening before the wedding, the Dupuises and the Reeds were sitting in a restaurant waiting for our oysters. Terry and I both—with martinis in hand—looked at each other and said "lechyd da!" Karen, Richard's wife, lit up and said, "Where did you get that expression?" Karen was Welsh and was shocked that here we were in Westport, Connecticut, toasting each other over oysters with martinis in Welsh.

I once went to New York to be interviewed by a potential client, Christine Quazzo. She was from London and involved in rather complicated litigation, part of which was taking place in Vermont and the rest in the Isle of Jersey and New York City. We met at her lawyer's office in New York. She was apparently satisfied with my credentials and my approach to the case and retained me to take on the Vermont end of the litigation. We finished the interview just about noon, and I suggested that we have some lunch. She was well acquainted with restaurants in London, but I had a bit of an upper hand in New York City. I suggested the Oyster Bar. We sat at the long white bar, and she had a gin and tonic while I had my usual martini. We both ordered oysters. The sharing of oysters cemented our relationship, and the litigation continued in one form or another for many years. As a result, we have shared meals in London, Vermont, and New York.

Our farm is an old farmhouse built in the 1850s of post and beam construction made from hand-hewn oak logs. It is a traditional small country farmhouse with a front porch. Along the front porch is a roof drip area. Joann and I decided that rather than use pea stone in the drip area we would fill it with oyster shells. It is great fun to sit on the porch with a martini in hand and a platter of oysters nearby, and after slurping them from the shell, you simply toss the empty shell into the drip bed. The drip bed is now piled high with oyster shells, and I joke that it represents a serious long-term investment. The wealth of the investment, of course, is the memories of many good times eating oysters and drinking martinis. I must confess that our drip edge of oysters off the porch has been somewhat disrupted by the free-roaming chickens in our yard that like nothing better than to scratch amongst them. They somehow manage to throw them for yards between their legs and scatter them on the lawn. Periodically, we try to rake the shells back into the immediate area, but there are still shells scattered willy nilly.

Oysters have often been the catalyst for bringing about good friendships. On one trip to Europe, which Joann and I made with our friends Kim and Sue Sparks, we planned to enjoy oysters in various spots on our itinerary. We arrived in Germany, and the first thing that Kim did was to insist that we go to a doctor he knew and have an injection of gamma globulin to prevent any problems that might arise from the different bacteria or other creatures we might meet while eating raw oysters in Europe. It had never occurred to us to think about potential dangers of eating raw oysters from different waters. It is the only time that I took a vacation trip where the first port of call was to expose my rump to a long needle administered by a German doctor.

One of my favorite days at the Oyster Bar was in early June when there is about a two-week period where they receive fresh herring. These herring are served raw with chopped onions in the same manner as they would be in Amsterdam. A good drink accompanying the herring is Genever Gin, a Dutch specialty. The herring are served at a small bar at the north end of the dining room; not the one where the oyster-shucking takes place. Here, I watched the bartender serve several people who were all enjoying the fresh herring. When I asked for a Genever Gin, an iced shot glass was put in front of me, and whenever it got low, the bartender filled it. All present were extolling to each other the marvelous experiences of eating this fresh herring. The conversation was jovial, and the making of new friends in the sharing of the herring was extraordinary.

When it came time to pay my bill, the bartender simply estimated the approximate amount of Genever Gin I drank and charged me a reasonable price. It was one of the few times in a public venue that I had been drinking with the freedom of a bottle and not counting individual drinks. I have always wanted to try to be in New York in those first few weeks of June to repeat the experience. This remains one of my most pleasant food memories.

Grand Central Station is the end terminal for trains coming from Chicago by way of Albany and down the Hudson River. If you reversed the route and started north and got off at Albany—actually Rensselaer across the river from Albany—you would find another of my favorite oyster bars. Jack's Restaurant at the end of State Street in Albany has been in operation since 1913 and owned by the same family: the Rosensteins. It is a wonderful old-world type of a restaurant. The waiters—and I do say waiters because for the many years that I patronized it, there were no waitresses—all wore the same uniform of short white jackets. It's a restaurant that caters to many of the powerful people who gather in the capital of New York State. Their menu includes not only oysters but lobster dishes, other seafood, and high-quality steaks and chops.

The first time I patronized Jack's was in 1956 when I was heading to Vermont from New York—traveling by bus. At that time, the bus terminal in Albany was at the end of State Street, just around the corner from Jack's. I was eighteen and found myself with a couple of hours between getting off the express bus from New York and waiting to change for a bus that would complete my journey to Middlebury. I walked around the corner, found Jack's, and for the first time in my life, I ordered swordfish. Of course, I had a martini while waiting for the swordfish to come. I was generally not a fish eater, and I can remember my delight in finding how good swordfish was when it is properly prepared. Since then, I have had many occasions to be in Albany—both for work and in transit to New York City. I have shared meals there with colleagues and friends, and I never pass up a chance to have a meal at Jack's, which always starts with oysters.

CHAPTER 2

Tobacco

I was raised in a tobacco-friendly era. Both my parents were cigarette smokers; my father smoked until his death at the age of eighty-four. I was never really interested in cigarettes, although I certainly tried them in my youth.

Andy Bean, my de facto big sister, was the daughter of the owner of Lake Dunmore Hotel—a summer hotel where my father was assistant manager. Together, we involved ourselves in all sorts of mischief around the hotel.

The hotel had a big wrap-around porch where the guests sat in old-fashioned rocking chairs, smoking and flicking the cigarette butts into a crushed rock drip ledge at the edge of the porch. Andy and I would gather the butts—mainly unfiltered Camel and Lucky Strikes cigarettes—strip the paper, and put the tobacco in a big paper bag. We would use this tobacco to roll our own cigarettes, sometimes with real rolling papers and sometimes with butcher paper. This was probably the strongest tobacco available, full of the butt ends of smoked, unfiltered cigarettes where the nicotine had concentrated. Fortunately, every time I tried to inhale our homemade cigarettes, I coughed. My experiments with smoking cigarettes were such that I can proudly say I didn't inhale—somewhat like Bill Clinton. This all came to an end when my mother found the brown paper bag with over a pound of tobacco hidden behind my dresser.

At an early age, I found that with cigars, I did not have to inhale. I smoked my first cigar at the age of twelve. It was a "Harvester," and I paid ten cents for it. In 1950, there was no age limit for buying tobacco. By the time I was sixteen, I was buying cigars by the box—usually Anthony and Cleopatra's (a Havana blend in a shape called Pats). I have continued smoking cigars to this day. I tried a pipe, but I found that even the attractive smell of good Turkish tobacco could not compensate for the hot smoke that burned my tongue. I soon rejected pipes as my nicotine of choice. While cigars are not directly connected to either breaking bread or drinking martinis, they have often been associated with good times and good friends, and are often shared after a meal over brandy and good conversation.

I started out on William Penn Cigars, which cost a nickel and a five pack for a quarter. At that early age, I was not a connoisseur of tobacco, and I thought I had found a bonanza with William Penn. Then I found Anthony and Cleopatra and left the nickel cigar behind me.

My relationship with my close friend Kim Sparks revolved, in part, around our mutual enjoyment of a good cigar. There was seldom a dinner at either of our houses that did not end up with a snifter of brandy and a good cigar.

I remember enjoying a cigar with Kim as we walked with our wives down the Pall Mall in London. It was late in the evening on our way back to our hotel from a play at the West End. We crossed paths with two young men who obviously had achieved certain financial success, judging by the cigars they were holding in their hands. They asked us if we had a cigar clipper. They brandished their large Havana (Churchill-shaped) cigars that must have cost them fifteen pounds each. When we told them that we did not have a clipper but that I had a jackknife, they asked if they could borrow it to clip their cigars. For those who are unfamiliar with cigars, one end is cut clean, meant to be lit, and the other is covered by a tobacco leaf cap. One has to remove the cap before lighting the cigar so it will draw. A good cigar is such that a nip with the front teeth will pull off the cap if a cigar cutter is not handy. The young men who accosted us knew nothing about smoking cigars, and certainly not cigars of this quality. They took my knife, and instead of trying to nip off the cap, they tried to cut off about a half inch at the base of the cigar. A cigar cutter, like a guillotine, cuts quite cleanly and cuts the end of a cigar at the tip end. However, trying to cut a half inch off with a jackknife is asking for a disaster and impossible to accomplish without having to make a mess of the cigar. The knife first has to cut through the wrapper and then the long leaf filler inside. Without asking us how to proceed, they started to cut half inch ends off, and when they saw they'd made such a mess of it, they complained that my knife was not sharp enough. I took my knife back, and Kim and I continued down the Pall Mall laughing at the experience— laughing at their inexperience but also with a sense of disappointment that such a good cigar, which was better than anything we were smoking, was being so callously treated.

I had invited a neighbor of ours, David Benedict, who had a summer home near our farm in Salisbury, Vermont, to join us for dinner at the Beaver Club in the Queen Elizabeth Hotel in Montreal. The Beaver Club, at that time, was one of Montreal's better restaurants. We had a wonderful dinner with all the trimmings. My friend was a Methodist minister who did not smoke. He did enjoy the wine we had with our meal. I said that I was going into the tobacco shop in the lobby to buy myself a good after-dinner cigar. As I had paid for the dinner, he insisted upon buying me the cigar. I suggested to him that I was going to buy a good Havana cigar that was quite expensive.

He, thinking an expensive cigar would probably cost at most two or three dollars, said that was no problem. I took him at his word and purchased a Havana Monte Cruz No. 2, which I still consider the world's best cigar. It cost $15.00, and as he took out his wallet to pay for it, there was a look of astonishment on his face when the clerk told him the price. He found it hard to believe that someone would pay $15.00 for the pleasure of burning tobacco.

In the years before the anti-tobacco crusades, you could smoke cigars in restaurants, and I often had a cigar after my dinner, accompanied by an after-dinner drink.

Joann and I met at the Waybury Inn in East Middlebury. (The Waybury Inn was the front-piece for the Bob Newhart Show) Often on our anniversary we would dine there, and one year when we had finished our dinner, I asked my wife if she would light my cigar for me. She happily (or unhappily) agreed to do so and was lighting the cigar when the waitress came with the usual request: "Would you like to see the dessert menu?" At that point, she looked at my wife and exclaimed, "Or are you having a cigar?" with an astonished look on her face.

One of the joys of having a friend like Kim Sparks who likes good cigars is that when you have an opportunity to obtain a good cigar, you always try to get two so that you can share them. Early in the 1960s the United States entered into an embargo prohibiting Cuban cigars from being imported to the U.S. Friends would sometimes smuggle some cigars in, and we were able to purchase some cigars in Canada that were true Havana's. If either of us had two Havana's, we saved them to share. Unfortunately, Kim passed away when he was seventy-six. It was not surprising that his widow turned over to me what cigars were left in his humidor. Because of the habit we had of sharing Havanas when we had them, there were none left. The gift still contained many good cigars, which I promptly smoked in his memory.

At my oldest son's wedding, in keeping with tradition, I put out a box of good cigars for anyone who wanted to enjoy a cigar after the reception dinner. They all went, although I think a few were taken by some of my son's friends for later use rather than being smoked at the reception itself.

In my reading of history, I have found many instances of prominent people smoking cigars—from Rudyard Kipling and Mark Twain to President Grover Cleveland. Cleveland was quoted as saying, "What this country needs is a good five-cent cigar." The comment was actually made by Thomas Riley Marshall, Vice President of the United States under Woodrow Wilson.

Kipling, in his poem "Betrothed," after praising many brands of cigars and comparing them with his intended, ended the poem with what would now be a politically-incorrect statement: "A woman is just a woman, but a good cigar is a smoke."

My practice took me to Jamaica once a year for negotiations involving harvest labor for Vermont apples. While enjoying a white rum at the beach bar at the Shaw Park Hotel in Ocho Rios, I would ask the bartender to bring over the humidor containing Royal Jamaican Cigars. I would select one to go with my white rum, both of which I would enjoy while looking over the Caribbean.

Upon returning from a fishing trip to the northwest territories at Kasba Lake, I discovered I had developed what is sometimes called the Holiday Heart, an irregular heartbeat. This turned out to be Atrial Fibrillation, and I put myself under the care of a cardiologist. After proceeding to get my heart back into an acceptable rhythm, I met with him and told him I was doing my best to improve my health. I said that I had given up caffeine, lost a few pounds, cut back on my salt, cut back on alcohol, carefully regulated my eating of greens which contained vitamin K (which has the potential for screwing up the blood thinner warfarin), and was even cutting down on my cigars. I will always love that doctor. After I finished my list of changes, he said, "Oh, cigars won't hurt you." This meeting took place after my meeting with a previous cardiologist, who, when I told him the same thing about my attempt to improve my health, suggested that he was concerned with my hydration and that I should probably have more salt in my diet and that I was probably eating too many greens because of potential warfarin screw-ups. Thus, collectively, my advice from cardiologists is: "Have more salt," "Eat less greens," and "Smoking cigars are ok." These are my type of cardiologists.

For thirty-five years, I held a license that allowed me to drive harness horses in pari-mutuel races. When I was in the sulky, I used to chew tobacco. I am a right-sided spitter. The right shoulder of my driving silks can testify to that.

Ordinarily I like smoking a cigar under circumstances where I can relax and enjoy sitting down, and I really don't enjoy chewing one while doing physical activities.

To those people who criticize my smoking cigars as dangerous to my health, I tell them they do not understand that I do it *for* my health. I often have long drives to or from court or am returning late in the evening after driving a race at Saratoga Raceway. I tell them my health is protected because cigars keep me awake, and the danger of falling asleep is a much greater threat to my health and others than smoking the cigar.

The anti-tobacco forces, mainly aimed at cigarettes, have made major changes in my smoking habits. When I first was appointed a commissioner on Uniform State Laws and attended the annual meeting, we were drafting the Uniform Probate Code. The insurance companies that issued fiduciary bonds were lobbying the commission to be sure we included fiduciary bond requirements in the proposed act. As a gesture of their good will, they had a box of La Corona Coronas on the hospitality table, which we were invited to take and smoke in the meetings. Likewise, when I first served in the House of Delegates of the American Bar Association or attended the annual meetings of the American Law Institute, smoking was allowed. On one occasion, I was sitting in the first row in the meeting of the House of Delegates and the TV press got a picture of me puffing on a cigar while listening to the debate. It made national TV, and I got kidded quite a bit. I used to smoke cigars in other meetings and, of course, in my office itself. Those days are gone.

I did get reprimanded on occasion. One time I especially remember. I had finished my shift as a bellhop at the Basin Harbor Club and was still in uniform. On the way back to the dormitory, there was an empty Adirondack chair on the lawn overlooking the harbor, and I decided to sit down and smoke a cigar. Bob Beach—the owner/manager—came by and told me that he did not think it was appropriate that I should be sitting in an Adirondack chair on the lawn while still in uniform smoking a cigar. His rebuke was good-natured, but from there on in I took off my uniform before I lit up.

My legal work had once taken me to Montreal. I had a young associate with me—a recent graduate from Yale Law School, Tony Patt. After we finished our work for the day, I took him to dinner at The Beaver Club. The Beaver Club had a history of being an exclusive organization for the Anglo-Canadians who both survived and exercised their control in the French-speaking Montreal. After having had a martini and a good steak, I asked the waiter to bring the humidor of Havana cigars so I might enjoy a good smoke to go with my brandy. Tony Patt declined to smoke a cigar, but that did not stop me from choosing a Monte Cruz No. 2—a torpedo-shaped cigar. The waiter took the cigar from the humidor, clipped its end, lighted a cedar taper, then, holding it in his hand, proceeded to light the cigar, rolling it with his fingers to make sure that the cigar took a good and even light. When he was satisfied that the cigar was burning properly, he handed it to me, and I had the pleasure of the first puff of a great cigar to compliment my brandy. It is hard to believe in today's non-smoking world that it was perfectly appropriate to light up a good cigar and enjoy it at the dinner table with an after-dinner digestive. Although I have enjoyed many cigars after a good dinner, this was the only time when I had a waiter light it for me and hand it to me after it was lit.

CHAPTER 3

Martinis

When I was eleven years old, I met Gabriel Garber. Gabe, his sister, Ellen, and his parents were guests at The Lake Dunmore Hotel on their first of many three-week vacations. As my father was assistant manager, our family had a table in the dining room. At that age, waiting for the waitress to bring our order was satisfied only by eating two saltines with a pad of butter in between them.

At lunch the first day the Garbers arrived, I noticed Gabe was sitting at a nearby table with his family. We eyed each other. After lunch, we got together and found out that both of us loved to fish. We spent most of the next three weeks inseparable, fishing, swimming, and hiking, or otherwise getting into trouble. As years passed, our friendship grew thicker and we began seeing each other at other times in addition to his family vacations. My family lived in Queens, and I learned the patterns of public transportation throughout the five boroughs of New York. Actually, four boroughs as I never really got to know Staten Island.

Gabe's family lived in Trenton, New Jersey, and in winter, we visited each other's homes. As we grew older, there were reasons for Gabe to come to New York City. When he did, we traveled into the city under my guidance of the New York subway system, pretending to be much more sophisticated than we were. Gabe, a year my senior, was the ringleader. On our escapades, we went into a piano bar in New York City. We were dressed in sport jackets with shirts and ties. Gabe ordered for the both of us (absinthe martinis). An absinthe martini is a regular gin martini with a dash of absinthe, giving it a liquorice taste. At that time, the drinking laws in New York allowed anyone eighteen or over to purchase alcohol legally. The reality was that if you were sixteen or so and had green cash with you there was no problem in getting served. I did not know what a martini was—much less what an absinthe martini was—but this was the beginning of a life-long relationship with that marvelous and crazy drink, the martini (not the absinthe).

Over the years, Gabe and I have shared martinis of many kinds in many places and in many sized glasses. Prior to one of his visits to Vermont, I had purchased a cocktail glass that would hold something close to a pint of liquid. On Gabe's arrival, I generously filled it with a well-shaken martini. He didn't come back for seconds.

Of all the martinis we drank together, one stands out in my mind. It was the worst martini I ever had and yet in some ways the best—at least from a story-telling standpoint. Gabe had a driver's license and access to his father's car when they were on vacation. I was working in the hotel dining room, and our adventures would usually start shortly after 8:00 pm, after I had finished my duties. One night we decided to take advantage of the New York State drinking laws. Vermont's drinking age was twenty-one and while it was not strictly enforced, it was a hell of a lot easier to get a drink in New York. We crossed the Champlain Bridge at Chimney Point and drove south towards Ticonderoga. About a half mile from the bridge on the left was the Trading Post. This was a bar where a great number of Vermont youths used to come, pay the dime toll to cross the bridge, and sit down to have a few. This particular night, we were still in our self-adopted sophisticated stage, and we arrived at the bar, found a table, and sat down. Joe, who was the proprietor and knew how to open a bottle of beer and pour a shot, came to our table. There were three of us, and we all ordered martinis. Joe was more interested in selling drinks than he was in figuring out exactly what a martini was. He appeared to be a bit puzzled by our order. I left our table to go to the men's room. On route as I passed the bar, I saw Joe working on the martinis. He took three cocktail glasses from a wooden rack above the bar, set them in line upon the bar, and took the bottom of his apron to wipe them. They obviously had not been used in a long time and had accumulated a combination of cigarette smoke and hamburger grease. After he set each wiped glass on the bar, he reached for a metal cocktail shaker. Then he looked on the shelf under the bar to find his bartender's handy book. A quick glance at the book told him that a martini contained both gin and vermouth. Not concerned with the proportions of either, Joe opened a bottle of non-descriptive gin and poured some into the shaker. Realizing that vermouth was much cheaper than gin, he poured in a great deal more vermouth than gin. Carefully, he shook the concoction and poured the contents into the recently wiped cocktail glasses. Apparently, he had heard about a lemon twist in a martini. But since he didn't have any lemon readily available, he decided a slice of lime would do just as well. Slices of lime were dropped into each glass. He poured the concoction into the three glasses, and the third glass came up short, so he topped it off with an open bottle of club soda retrieved from under the bar. Nowhere in my experience have I ever drunk a martini that was 2-1 vermouth over gin with a sliced lime and topped with club soda. We may have thought we were sophisticated drinking martinis, but we decided not to challenge his bartending abilities, and we managed to down them. We ordered something else for the second round.

***

Martinis were the drink of choice for both Randy and myself after what turned out to be an amazing day. The Randy I am talking about is Randy Quaid, star of the film "Christmas Vacation." He and his wife, Evi, and my wife, Joann, were being treated to dinner at Tourterelle's Restaurant just north of Middlebury. The host for our dinner was a young woman, a stringer for one of the major TV networks. I had arranged to give her an exclusive interview with Randy at our office in Middlebury. This was after a long day in court in St. Albans. I agreed for Randy to have an exclusive with her as she was the most pleasant and least aggressive of the paparazzi who followed Randy that day.

The background of that day began five years earlier when the Quaids were charged with unlawful trespass and malicious mischief in connection with their entering a home in Santa Barbara. The Quaids had purchased the home many years before. They claimed to still own the house but were not in possession of it as the result of a forged deed. That deed is the centerpiece of continuing litigation in California.

Randy had been scheduled to receive a Canadian award for his acting accomplishments. He and Evi left Santa Barbara for Vancouver to receive the award. Once in Canada, they found out that arrest warrants had been issued against them for the alleged trespass into the home they claimed to still own. Because of his celebrity status, the entire matter grew out of hand. Attempts were made to extradite the Quaids back to the United States and that failed. The California warrants called for a ridiculous bail of $500,000 and justifiably frightened the Quaids. All the brouhaha resulted in the Quaid's remaining in Canada for five years before attempting to reenter the United States. They finally attempted entry through Highgate, Vermont; Vermont being Evi's home. On crossing the border, the border police learned that there was an outstanding warrant in California calling for their extradition. They were placed under arrest.

Evi was raised in Middlebury, and I knew her father partially because he was my son's Russian teacher at Middlebury Union High School. He called me, and I agreed to represent Evi and Randy in connection with the extradition proceedings. The first step was a hearing in St. Albans, Vermont, the shire town of Franklin County. The hearing was to review bail as they waited on an extradition hearing. The papers calling for a forced return to California were presented to the court with Judge Alison Arms presiding. In an open-court proceeding, the judge dismissed two of the claims for extradition based on the fact that there was not sufficient information to justify holding them as there was a lack of showing of probable cause. The third claim charged them with failing to appear at a hearing. This was enough, she indicated, to hold them to wait for extradition. She then went on to set bail at $50,000. The courtroom was filled not only with the local press but the national and international media looking for a story involving a well-known celebrity.

Disappointed in the outcome, I went downstairs to the holding cell to talk to Randy and about how to arrange for the $50,000 bail. As I was talking to Randy, the sheriff entered the cell and said that the court wanted to see me in chambers immediately. I had no idea what this was about nor any reason for its immediacy. I left Randy, telling him I would be back shortly. When I got upstairs to the space outside the judge's chambers, I met with State's Attorney Jim Hughes. He shrugged his shoulders and said that he had no idea why we were being summoned. We entered chambers, and the judge was sitting behind her desk with Randy's file in front of her. She indicated for us to sit down and then proceeded to tell us that after open court she had gone back to her chambers and decided to once more review the documents.

She noticed that the warrant on its face indicated that the charge for failure to appear was dated before the date they were supposed to appear, and, therefore, had to be invalid. She told us she was going to go back in court, reverse her ruling, and release both the Quaids.

I did not have time to go back to Randy in his cell before court was called to order. The press had already started to disperse and call in their story. When they got news that there was more going on, there was a mad scramble to get back into the courtroom. I was standing at the counsel table when Randy was brought through the side prisoner's door, and all I could say to him was to remain cool; it was good news. He shuffled over to me, wearing leg shackles and handcuffs, and we waited for the court to take the bench. Judge Arms came out, announced her change of decision, and ordered the sheriffs to immediately release Randy from his shackles. The sheriffs happily obliged, and in open court, unlocked the handcuffs, unlocked the leg shackles, and wished Randy good luck.

By this time, a large crowd had assembled in the back of the courtroom and in the hallway. As we walked out of the courtroom, the reporters were asking for comments from both myself and Randy. Randy said, "I feel so good about this I could kiss his balding head," then returned his gaze to my thinning hair. We got into my car, left to pick up his belongings that had been left at the jail, and then went to pick up Evi, who was being held in another county. There was a crowd of people on the streets in Saint Albans as we left, all waving good cheers to Randy.

All the major networks were looking for interviews. We declined them all, except I had time to tell the young woman from the Plattsburgh affiliate to meet me at my office in Middlebury at 6:00 pm and she would have her interview. After the filmed interview was over, the young reporter called and got authorization to take us all out to dinner. I made reservations at the best restaurant in Middlebury. This resulted in our trip to Tourterelle, where we enjoyed martinis accompanied by oysters, a steak, and finally after dinner a "Cardenal Mendoza" Spanish brandy. I felt good about giving a young woman reporter—a stringer for the network—an exclusive. It would look good on her resume.

At the restaurant, I noticed for the first time the horrible cost of privacy a celebrity goes through when they appear in public. All of the other dining guests—many of whom I knew—recognized Randy and, while they were polite enough not to interrupt our dinner, we could feel their interest in his being there. The kitchen staff was looking through the windows and pointing towards our table. This must happen every day of their lives when they appear in public. No wonder they cherish their limited privacy.

Over the years, I have handled many cases that have received publicity in Vermont papers and even on a couple of occasions the New York Times, however, I have never before had my picture appear in a London tabloid. People thought I had done an amazing job in getting them both released, when the truth was, they were released because a good judge under pressure went through the paperwork and found a discrepancy and acted on it.

Every summer through college and my first year in law school, I worked at Lake Dunmore Hotel as the relish boy. As a relish boy, I served jams and jellies at breakfast; pickles, olives and other relishes at lunch and dinner. My tips averaged about a dollar a week from about 150 guests. It was the most lucrative job in the hotel, next to the chef, and paid for a lot of my education. The University of Chicago's school year was four quarters of ten weeks each. As a result, the fall quarter did not start until very early in October. Lake Dunmore Hotel closed on Labor Day and, thus, I had the month of September to try and earn some more money toward college expenses. Fortunately, the Basin Harbor Club in Ferrisburgh, Vermont, did not close until what was then Columbus Day Weekend. They lost a lot of their summer employees around Labor Day when most students went back to college. I was always welcomed to fill one of the vacancies for the month of September. Over the years, I did virtually everything from social director, waterfront director, bellhop, to anything else where help was needed. No matter what my job was, I wrote the in-house daily newsletter. While I was social director, on off time, I could take advantage of the resort's amenities, including the golf course.

Once each week, Bob Beach, who was part owner and manager of the resort and the son of A. P. Beach, the founder of the resort, would hold a cocktail party for all its guests. As social director, it was my job to coordinate this function. Only two drinks were served—martinis and manhattans. The martinis, of course, were gin martinis as they were the only ones that people thought about in those days. We had two large punch bowls, both filled with ice, and one we used for making martinis by pouring in several bottles of gin and a small amount of vermouth. The other bowl was filled with blended whisky and a heavier proportion of sweet vermouth. Cocktails were ladled out from either punch bowl into a martini glass that either had an olive or a cherry in it—depending on which bowl was used. As social director, I, of course, had to participate in the consumption of the cocktails. It was not the toughest part of my job. It is interesting to reflect that such a function today would probably be limited to red and white wine with no spirits in sight. Back then it was all spirits, and no one ever thought of having wine at a cocktail party.

One does not usually think of martinis being made other than one at a time. The idea of a pitcher of martinis is something that you don't see very often today. However, back then that was not unusual.

Vermont was still a town-option state in the 50s and as Ferrisburgh had not elected to allow the sale of liquor, the resort did not have any bar. Thus, the guests had their cocktails in their cottages or rooms or at the weekly cocktail party thrown by management where the alcohol was gifted and not sold.

When there was any type of meeting or convention function, the alcohol had to be supplied by the organizers of the function rather than the Basin Harbor Club itself.

One fall, the Vermont Bar Association had its September meeting at the Harbor. I was drafted to be a bartender. I can remember thinking at the time that I had never seen so few men drink so much whisky in so short a period of time (all spirits and no wine).

It was all men as I did not see any of Vermont's few female lawyers in attendance. Drinking was a serious pastime for a lot of the lawyers in the 50s. With a sense of efficiency, I made a pitcher of martinis and set it on the bar to use for anyone requesting a martini. Charles Brown, the Speaker of the Vermont House of Representatives, had a law practice in Brandon. He had decided that over the years he had had enough to drink and now at functions drank only water. He was sufficiently gruff, and he would not ask for a glass of water but just help himself to it. On this particular evening, he approached the bar, and I asked him if I could get him a drink. He grunted at me, reached for a glass, and, thinking he was pouring himself a glass of water, poured himself a highball glass of well-iced martinis. Given his lack of response to me, I said nothing as I saw the surprised expression on his face when he took a large swallow of what was not his expected water.

A martini is supposed to be a generous drink. I try to avoid restaurants that serve a stingy martini and go out of my way to patronize establishments that serve a generous drink. Recently one of my favorite restaurants that serves a generous martini is The Rotisserie in South Burlington, Vermont. They also do it with a bit of ceremony. Whether it is Sean, the owner, or Sam, a generous bartender, they serve the martini by bringing empty, chilled cocktail glasses each with an olive on a tray to the table. They have a stainless-steel shaker filled with well-chilled and very dry martinis. The glasses are placed on the table, and Sean or Sam will pour from the shaker until they are filled to the brim. It is suggested that you take a first sip as they wait to pour a divided into the glasses. They have even been known to carry a straw to facilitate the first sip. This mini ceremony and the conversation that goes with it are one of the nicest ways to continue the martini's reputation as a generous drink.

CHAPTER 4

Fire & Grouse

In 1992, we suffered a fire at our home. It was February, and the waterline from the house to the barn had frozen. A young man who was working for us decided to try and thaw out the waterline. Unfortunately, the way he thought of thawing the waterline was applying a small blowtorch to the shut off valve on the side of the house. The flame of the blowtorch penetrated the outside wall into the post and beam construction and set fire to the accumulated dust between the outside wall and the plaster on the inside.

At the time I was in court in Alaska, when I was handed a note by the court bailiff that my wife was trying to reach me, and I returned her call at the first opportunity. Little did I expect Joann to tell me that our house was on fire. Fortunately, the Salisbury Volunteer Fire Department was there and controlled the fire. While there was substantial damage done inside the walls, we lost virtually no personal property. It did, however, require stripping down the walls in the old part of the house. The reconstruction gave us an opportunity to make some improvements, including an eight-foot extension to the front of the house—giving us a bigger kitchen and a mud room. The fire was the catalyst for many stories.

My wife has always made my ties, and each year I would receive two or three for Christmas and sometimes one or two for my birthday. The claim manager for the local Middlebury Cooperative Insurance Company approached me concerning the dry-cleaning bill that was incurred by having all our clothing dry cleaned due to the smoke damage. He looked at me and said, "Peter—one hundred and thirty-seven ties."

After resolving a criminal trial favorably (the defendant received no extra time as opposed to the possibility of a life sentence), the jury, who had been sequestered and locked together in a hotel for over a week, were assembled on the front steps of the Franklin County courthouse to say goodbye to each other after a week of sharing all meals (but no martinis). I came out the side door, and one of the jurors waved and beckoned me over. I was greeted with smiles and told that they had enjoyed my ties.

A representative of the insurance company was at our house while the firemen were still on the roof. He wrote a check to my wife for $10,000 on the spot to make sure she had cash to deal with whatever was necessary in taking care of the immediate needs of the house after the fire. The advantage of a local company.

As a result of the fire, we were forced to seek temporary lodgings. Fortunately, our good friends Kim and Sue Sparks had room for us. Even better, they were planning to leave for Europe for an extended period as Kim Sparks, a professor of German at Middlebury College, was scheduled for a stay in Mainz, Germany, to head up Middlebury College's off-campus German language school. We got to serve as their house sitter, which coincided with our need for temporary housing.

Our close friendship had flourished over the years, and we regularly shared meals and libations (and cigars). The food memories of sharing meals over that period of time are memorable. Our decent-sized wine cellar escaped serious damage from the fire, but we thought it prudent to make use of it as soon as possible. The best of the wines we transported to the Sparks' house in Cornwall, where each night we enjoyed them. As we were the guests in the house, I felt it upon myself to bring home some very special groceries. We had lobster at least once a week. I raided our freezers, which had survived the fire, for some fine cuts of meat. On our farm, we grow beef, lamb, and pork and have a chest freezer for each. We dined well, with all dinners being preceded by very dry Beefeater martinis with a twist of lemon. Joann and I continued these rituals even after the Sparks took off for Germany.

When they returned, we found out that the insurance policy had a provision to reimburse us for the cost of displaced housing. We were modest in our demands, but it still amounted to us receiving a check in the amount of $2,200. The Sparks were reluctant to take rent money from us, claiming that we had done them a favor by house sitting. Thus a joint decision; the money should be used for a special long weekend trip for the four of us to Quebec City. Reservations were made at the Chateau Frontenac, and on a Friday morning we took off for the north. On our route, we stopped in the Town of Johnson at a little but very good diner. We had a good meal, and the bill was so modest that we joked we would have ample funds for the trip to Quebec City and would probably have money left over. We were wrong.

A mutual friend of ours and the Sparks was George Jaeger. George had served as a diplomat in residence at Middlebury College after he retired from the State Department. One of his jobs in the State Department had been chief consul in Quebec City. It was a difficult post as it was in the time of René Levesque and the movement to withdraw the French-speaking province of Quebec from the rest of Canada. As George knew the city so well, we sought him out and asked for his advice on restaurants in Quebec. He told us the name of what he considered to be the best restaurant in Quebec. It was on the second floor of a building in the heart of Quebec City. We made a reservation for four. On arrival, we were seated in a large dining room with well-set tables and large spaces between them. This was the setting for one of the memorable meals of my life—but not because of the food (which was quite good, I indulged in one of my favorites—sweet breads). Shortly after we ordered, a party of four was seated at the next table over. It was a couple with two children. The father in the family was casually dressed with a large gold medallion hanging around his neck, emphasized by the showing of skin through his open-neck sport shirt. His wife was dressed as what I can only describe as an old man's wet dream. They had with them two children—one about eight; a young girl who was dressed all in white in what looked like a confirmation dress. She was apparently in charge of their two-year-old, the fourth member of the party. The two-year-old was the epitome of what is often called the "terrible twos." He was constantly noisy, sometimes yelling, sometimes crying. He was not the companion one wants for a quiet, quality, and expensive dinner.

At one point, Kim, in his frustration, called the waiter over and said in perfect French, "Je voudrais changer mon ordre. (I desire to change my order). Je désire un enfant rôti (I would like a roasted child)." The waiter was taken back for a second and then a smile spread across his face. He left the dining room and soon all the staff in the kitchen were looking out of the window in the kitchen door to see who had the sense of humor that engendered such a remark. They gave us the thumbs up sign. From there on, we tolerated the noise, but the service we got was excellent and with a smile that made the entire occasion a memorable (and joyful) happening.

George Jaeger was born in Vienna—his father was Jewish. He immigrated to the United States with his father before the Nazi invasion. His father was an accomplished artist, and he became the lead illustrator for Hallmark Cards. At age nineteen, George entered the United States Army, and because of his ability to speak German, he was assigned to intelligence duty and often sent to the front line. He was in Czechoslovakia a few days after VE Day. He had some free time and liberated a bicycle, going for a leisurely ride on a back road in the countryside. As he rounded a corner of the road, he ran head-on into a German Panzer division. He was not sure what to do. He had three choices: 1) to turn and run and probably get shot in the back; 2) to stop and reach for his rifle—with no chance of success; or 3) to keep on pedaling as if nothing were happening. He took the last choice. George was stopped by a German soldier, who at gun point told him to stay right where he was. Soon a senior officer, a colonel appeared. He came forward and said, "Are you an American soldier?" Not knowing what the result of his answer would be, he answered in German that he was. The colonel abruptly exclaimed, "I wish to surrender my troops to a soldier of the United States Army." George then realized that the division was trying to outrun Russian troops who were on their trail so that they would become prisoners of the American Army and escape being sent to a gulag in Siberia. He accepted the colonel's offer and asked for some proof to take back to his superiors. The colonel handed him his Luger pistol. George then peddled his bicycle back to the base and reported to his sergeant. The sergeant, convinced he was joking, in no uncertain terms told him he was confined to his barracks and to get the hell out of his sight. George took it upon himself to ignore the sergeant's order and was finally able to see the U.S. colonel in charge. He told him that a German panzer division had just surrendered to him. The colonel—disbelieving him—made some unfriendly comments, at which point George produced the gun. George related what had happened, and the colonel's attitude instantly changed. He ordered George to go back to his barracks and stay there. He took the revolver from George and headed out to meet the German colonel, where he took full credit for the surrender.

Besides the restaurant George recommended, we had several good meals in Quebec City. One I remember involved seafood and a bottle of Pouilly Fumé. Either the wine was great or the atmosphere made it seem so as I always remember it was the best Pouilly Fumé I ever had. As a result, Pouilly Fumé is still my favorite white burgundy.

Another night we ventured down into the old town in Quebec and found a small restaurant. On the menu was an extraordinary piece of meat. It was a tenderloin de cheval (horse) served with a green Madagascar pepper sauce. It will go down as one of the four best servings of meat I've ever had.

While in Quebec, we also did a little shopping in antique shops, and I purchased two things. One was a crystal chandelier for our rebuilt house that still hangs in our dining room. The other was a print found in a small antique shop in an undramatic frame. The print is of a commissioned uniformed officer of the Grand Army of the Republic hunting partridge with a guide while a non-commissioned soldier is waiting in a wagon. As two partridges rise in front of setters on point, and the union officer fires his gun, dropping one. As a long-time hunter of partridge, I treasure the print, and it hangs in a place of honor in our home today.

To a Vermonter, a ruffed grouse is known as a partridge, and when it is on the table, it is the most delicious fowl that one could ever taste. For it to be at its best it must be aged properly. By aging properly, I mean that it should be hung for three to four days before it is plucked and dressed. Bill Rule, a close friend, had a different view at the beginning of our hunting friendship. He felt the bird should be dressed as soon as possible and not hung. On a hunt, he bagged a bird and field dressed it immediately. I had a bird at home that had been hanging for four days. We went back to my farm and plucked both birds and had a cook-off. After tasting both birds, Bill became a proponent of hanging birds. The meat from a partridge with a bountiful white breast, as well as darker legs and thighs, is absolutely extraordinary, with a wonderful texture.

There are many times when sharing partridge has provided a very special meal for me.

One such meal was when I received a call from Jhonas, a chef from Iceland whom I had met on a salmon fishing trip. He was visiting New York, and while there gave me a call. I suggested that he fly up and join us for a couple of days. He did. I picked him up at the airport and brought him home. We were having a roast partridge, and as I prepared to put it in the oven, he turned to me and said, "Peter, no—breast down—you must cook it breast down." Previous to that, I had always put the bird in the oven with the breast up. He explained that by cooking it breast down, the juices flowed into the breast and kept it moist and that you could turn it just before it was ready to take from the oven and leave it for a short time in a high temperature oven and brown it. I have since cooked partridge and all other fowl, even turkeys, breast down. The best part of that dinner, however, was the fact that Joann had made a pâté, which included the finger-like pieces from the inside part of the breast of a Canada goose. It also had the skin of the goose spread over the top of the pâté, giving it a special appearance. It took about three days to make. It was the only time in our lives Joann ever made this, and it was magnificent. It was especially fun because our guest Jhonas recognized both the quality of the pâté, and that it had been several days in the making. It was a pleasant surprise to him to have such a dish in rural Vermont, which he knew had been prepared before we knew he was coming.

Stuart Frum and his wife, Betty, visited us one Sunday for an early-afternoon dinner. At the table, Stuart told me that while driving from his home in Westport in NY, just across Lake Champlain, he hit a grouse flying across the road. Knowing my penchant for grouse, he said, "I almost stopped and picked it up to bring it to you." I told him he should be ashamed of himself to let good meat like that go to waste. We all laughed, and the conversation continued on to other subjects.

As Stu and Betty left, I walked out with them. As we approached their car, I noticed what looked like the head of a bird hanging down from behind his car's radiator. I pointed to it, and on investigation, it indeed was a grouse. When he had hit the bird, it somehow had fallen behind the radiator, and was still whole, with only its head hanging down. He started laughing. Unknown to me, he had stopped at a car wash on the way over. "Now I understand why the attendant kept pointing at my front end as we were going through the carwash."

I removed the grouse, hung it for three days, and eventually enjoyed a good meal from it. Certainly, it is the only grouse I've ever eaten that has been thoroughly washed before plucking.

CHAPTER 5

Gabe Garber

Shortly after Joann and I were married, Gabe Garber, my oldest friend, was studying in Boston to become an orthodontist. He would come up and visit us on weekends, and his trips often included John Streetz, a former teacher of his at the George School, a Quaker School. John was an African American about 6'4" and a former world class sprinter. He also loved to fish. On a bright sunny Saturday, we decided to go trout fishing on the east side of our nearest mountain where a good brook ran along Vermont Route 125. The brook empties into the White River, which in turn empties into the Connecticut River, which in turn empties into Long Island Sound. Brooks on the west side of the mountain make their way to Lake Champlain, eventually emptying out through Quebec into the Gaspé.

As we drove up the mountain approaching Middlebury College's Breadloaf Campus and Middlebury College Snowbowl, a porcupine was crossing the road in front of us. I immediately pulled the car to the side of the road and got out holding a pounder—a 16-ounce Budweiser. I grabbed a stick and hit the porcupine across the nose, killing it. This may seem a bit uncouth, but this was shortly after a time when the State of Vermont offered a thirty-five-cent bounty for each porcupine killed, upon presentation of both ears to the town clerk. The bounty was thought justified because of the damage porcupines did debarking trees. More important to me was the fact that I knew a porcupine liver was a great delicacy. It really is. I took my knife, disemboweled the porcupine, took out its liver, and with one hand with a knife and a dripping liver in it and my beer still in the other hand, I returned to the car. Polly Brown stepped out on the porch of her nearby house and inquired, "Can I be of any help?" I said, "No, we are just getting some porcupine liver." She blanched and hurried back into the house, slamming her door. I was assailed by my two companions as I opened the car door as a decadent meat hunter with no principles. They may have been right.

When we returned home, I sautéed the liver and served it with fresh scallions. Then everybody agreed that it was worth it. However, the tag of "decadent meat hunter" was attached to me by my friends ever after.

Gabe Garber accused me of being such a meat hunter that I would shoot a pink plastic flamingo on someone's lawn and take it home for dinner. I remembered his accusation some years later at my oldest son's wedding. The wedding was held on our farm, and we had a rehearsal dinner there the night before. Gabe was in attendance. I had purchased a plastic pink flamingo lawn ornament and set it in my back garden. As the group gathered, the party became a little livelier—prompted by martinis. Suddenly I looked out the window and shouted, "It's here." I got a 20-gauge shotgun, put in a shell, opened the window, and shot the plastic flamingo. After that I yelled, "I got it, I got it." I went out the back door and retrieved it in front of the wedding party and gave it to Gabe, suggesting that perhaps he would like it for dinner. He kept that flamingo for I don't know how many years.

Gabe has played other major roles in my life. I had been raised in the Episcopal Church and was a server carrying the crucifix in the opening sessions of church services. One might have thought I was thinking of going into the priesthood. When Joann and I married, we joined the Episcopal church in Middlebury; although I had no literal belief in the actual theological teachings of the church, I felt it was a worthwhile part of the community. When it came time to baptize our first son, Fritz, we wanted Gabe to be his godfather. Of all the people I knew, Gabe was the one I would have trusted to raise our son if something had happened to Joann and myself. I learned there was a problem. He was Jewish. Russ Ellis, the local priest, came out and explained to me that he could not be the godfather because he could not in good conscience say the Apostles Creed as it required that he say he believed in Jesus Christ the Son of God. I took that to heart and realized that I could not say that in good faith either, and I have never darkened an Episcopal church or any other church for purposes of worship since.

Another story concerning Gabe involved a night when he was visiting us at our camp on Lake Dunmore, and we drove to East Middlebury for dinner at the Waybury Inn. The Waybury Inn is where I had first met Joann in 1958. Returning to Lake Dunmore, we encountered a herd of about twenty Holstein heifers in the middle of the road. They had escaped a pasture and were a long way from home. We were relaxed after a martini at dinner, and we decided that we would help the farmer round them up and get them back into the pasture. I was walking next to the farmer who welcomed our help, trying to make pleasant conversation. I asked him if any of the heifers were bred yet. His comment was "I sure as hell hope so—I got a bull in here." Just at that point, I looked over and saw Gabe standing behind a small tree with only a four-inch diameter, looking at the bull while the bull snorted and pawed the ground. Gabe was talking very softly, repeating the phrase "nice cow" over and over. I don't know if the tone of his voice worked or whether the bull just got tired of it and walked away. In any case, there was no disastrous result.

CHAPTER 6

Introduction to Travel

On February 1, 1965, I finished two terms plus as State's Attorney of Addison County. When I had started the job in November of 1960, it was a half-time job that paid $2,000 a year plus $400 towards expenses. It gave me a free office in the courthouse, and it paid the basic charges for my phone. The real advantage of the job was that it allowed me to build up a practice with the other half of my time. At that time, the minimum wage was fifty cents an hour, and a good worker earned a dollar and a half an hour. Lawyers charged ten dollars an hour.

By 1965, my private practice had grown and I thought I could make a living as a sole practitioner. In the four plus years that I had served as State's Attorney of Addison County, we never took a real vacation. Joann and I married on July 4, 1960 in San Diego, California, and we immediately came back to Middlebury to start my campaigning for State's Attorney. I was running against the incumbent and another lawyer, and the only hope I had at winning was to campaign vigorously and meet as many people in the county as possible. This meant spending most of the day driving from house to house, trying to meet people one-on-one. In the early evenings, Joann and I would pick a village and go down the streets, house by house, to introduce ourselves and indicate that I was running for State's Attorney, hoping that I would have their vote. The campaign was successful. In the Republican primary where I had my name on the ballot, I beat the incumbent by a two-to-one margin and the other candidate by a seven-to-one margin. I also won the Democratic nomination by write-in's, thereby virtually ensuring me of a victory in November.

The reason this is all relevant to the topic at hand is that I had never in my entire life been outside the United States, with the exception of a day trip from San Diego to Tijuana, Mexico, the week before our wedding. On that trip to Tijuana, I tried a half a sheep's head and a shot of tequila taken with salt and lime, both for the first time. The next time I had a sheep's head was many years later in a *parador* in Spain.

Joann, on the other hand, was a daughter of a naval officer and had been raised around the world. She went to high school for four years in four different countries. In her Christmas stocking in 1964, I put applications for passports and two round-trip tickets to Paris. In February of 1965, we took our first real vacation—a three-week excursion to Europe. At that time, you could buy a round-trip ticket to a point in Europe and have as many stopovers in different airports as you desired with the flight charges being calculated only on the farthest point to the east that you went. This trip was a tremendous growing experience for me and resulted in many good meals shared with old friends of Joann's living in Europe. It also set a pattern for our love of travel.

Our first stop was Paris. Joann spent a year there in high school and another year at the Middlebury College program at the Sorbonne getting her master's degree in French. She spoke beautiful French with a Parisian accent, and this allowed us to be received in a manner that would not have been afforded to many American tourists.

Two stories come to mind from our stay in Paris. First, we were dining out with friends in a quite nice French bistro. On the menu was steak tartare. I had never had steak tartare, but I was convinced that I would love it. When the waiter came, I tried in obviously English-laced French to order steak tartare. The waiter, realizing I was a tourist, wanted to make sure that I knew that steak tartare was raw beef and not a cooked steak. I expect others before me had been surprised when the raw beef was served to them. My wife spoke out and explained to the waiter that I knew exactly what I was ordering and that was what I wanted. The waiter turned around, threw up his hands walking away, and was heard to say, "No wonder the English win in football." I learned the next day that England had just beaten France in a soccer competition and my English-laced French was so bad that he thought that I was British.

The second memory comes from the fact that both Joann and I had limited experience with but a great affection for opera. We wanted to see an opera and see the famed Paris Opera house. We did not really care what the opera was. Everywhere we tried to get tickets we were informed that they were sold out. We came back to our hotel, the Hotel Roblin, and asked our concierge if there was any chance of getting tickets to the opera the next night. He said, "Ah, you want to see Callas, eh?" At that time, I really did not know who Maria Callas was. He said, "It will be very difficult, but I will see what I can do." He came through.

We had two seats dead center in the first balcony rows one and two, one seat behind the other. By the time we arrived at the opera house, we had learned more about Callas. She was going to sing one of her great roles, Tosca. There was another young couple in the box with us, and we became acquainted during the course of the opera. To say that the opera was magnificent would be an understatement. We suggested to our seat mates at the close of the opera that the four of us go down to Les Halles for a bowl of the traditional onion soup. It was the first time I had ever gone out to eat after a theatrical performance, and it set a pattern for the rest of my life. There is nothing I like better than a quiet dinner after the excitement of a great operatic or theatrical experience. That night the onion soup lived up to its reputation.

This trip involved a number of gastronomic firsts for me. From Paris we went on to Rome and Naples. In Rome, Joann visited an old friend she had from high school, Lola Nunziante, and her husband, a successful manufacturer of fine quality Italian china. They took us to a restaurant famous for its wild game. There, for the first time as an appetizer, I had wild boar sausage. It was good, but the name was more exciting than the sausage itself. For a second course, we had something I had never had before, and I have never had since. It was a serving of wild songbirds that had been captured somewhere in Italy. I do not know what kind of birds they were, and as I look back, as interesting as it sounded then and as interesting as it tasted, it is not something I would ever think of repeating.

From Rome, we went on to Naples. Joann and I were staying at the Excelsior Hotel, which I remember well because the starched sheets felt like you were sleeping on sandpaper. Next to the hotel there was a small restaurant. Joann and I went in and ordered a traditional Italian meal based upon our knowledge of American-Italian restaurants. At the next table there were four people having a dish consisting of a pot of small octopi. They noticed me staring at the pot, and they had great smiles on their faces as they offered to share a taste. I readily accepted and have loved all forms of squid and octopus since.

It was on to Denmark, where we were to meet up with Kirsten McEdwards. Kirsten lived in Middlebury, and it so happens she was back visiting her family in Denmark at the same time we were in Europe. Kirsten was married to Foster McEdwards, who was a pilot she had met at Tivoli Gardens, fell in love with and married within a matter of a couple of weeks before following him to Egypt on one of his jobs. The McEdwards were good friends in Middlebury and remained so for over a half a century.

Kirsten gave us a tour of her hometown. We went to the school, where the principal and teachers fawned over Kirsten, who was obviously one of their favorite students. We had dinner at her family's home, and her mother and I got along quite well, and after dinner we both smoked cigars.

The next day, Kirsten took us up to the Jutland Peninsula to a restaurant on the North Sea. It was a meal I will never forget. It started out with a platter of cold fish. This was followed by a platter of hot fish. The third course was cold meat. The fourth course was hot meat. The fifth course was a platter of cheeses. The sixth course was an assortment of sweets, and the seventh course some fresh fruit. All of these were accompanied by large quantities of Carlsberg Beer and many shots of Aquavite. Joining us for this meal was Kristen's brother, Hans. Hans later settled in Thule, Greenland, where he had his own jewelry shop. He remarked that during his lifetime he had eaten all the things we had that day but never all at once. The sharing of the meat and libations took close to four hours.

After that, we took a walk, climbed a lighthouse on the edge of the North Sea, and then returned home to get ready for our flight the next day. Kirsten insisted upon driving us to the airport. We got a late start, and Kirsten took shortcuts to the airport, which I recall included farm roadways through the middle of cropped fields. We arrived as the last passenger was getting on the bus to take them out to the plane on the runway. We yelled. They stopped. They let us on, and we made it. This was the last plane—as a matter of fact it was the only plane—that day from her hometown to Copenhagen and then for us on to London.

Foster was a pilot extraordinaire. He flew with the Flying Tigers over the hump to Burma for Chenier towards the end of World War II. His travels have taken him all over the world, and on many occasions he flew assignments for companies connected to the CIA. In the early 1960s, he was offered a job to map Afghanistan. He asked me to come along as his ground man. My job would have been to make sure that at any time his plane took off, there was at least one Russian and one Afghani national, as well as an American, on board, thus guaranteeing that it would not be shot down. I declined the offer, and as it turned out, the job evaporated for Foster as well.

For a period of years, he flew a four-engine propeller airplane for the International Shoe Company. The plane was fitted out with the latest machinery for making shoes and flew for demonstrations worldwide. I would often get a call from Foster, who was in some part of the world with his plane undergoing certain repairs, asking me to handle certain matters for him either at home or in connection with his current situation.

I handled a civil lawsuit for him once against Canada's Northern Telecom. Foster had been hired as the company's chief pilot based upon a gentleman's agreement with its president that the job would last for at least three years. The president reneged on his agreement. It did not take a Vermont jury long to award Foster the damages he was asking for.

In London, Joann and I booked a table at the classic English restaurant Simpsons on the Strand. The waiter brought out a trolley, on top of which was a silver-covered platter. The waiter pushed back the cover, exposing a roast rib of beef. He then proceeded to slice the roast at the table. It was not only a wonderful piece of beef, but it was a type of service that I had never experienced before.

While in London, I could not get enough of the English breakfasts, which included English bacon, which comes from a different part of the pig than American bacon and is much meatier and broader in its thin slices. It also included a fried egg, blood pudding, baked beans, and sausages (bangers), as well as fried bread. I have always been a breakfast eater, and this fits into my idea of what an ideal breakfast should be.

While I had never been to horse races, I had always been fascinated by horse racing. Even as a small child, I can remember reading the New York Daily Mirror on a daily basis and making hypothetical bets. I can also recall, in 1947, listening on the radio to a call of Assault winning the Kentucky Derby and then again hearing Citation winning the 1948 Derby. Both horses went on to win the Triple Crown. So in London, I had a chance not only to see racing but to see jump racing, both hurdles and steeplechases, at Kempton Park. I had always enjoyed horses as a child after working in a riding stable barn in exchange for free rides.

Joann and I boarded a train in London, which stopped right at Kempton Park. On route, we were seated in a European-style compartment where there were two benches, each holding three people facing each other. At one end, a door opened to a corridor, and on the other end was another door opening directly to the platform. We sat together on one side of the compartment. On the other side there was a rather distinguished-looking gentleman with a young man who appeared to be his son. They were diligently reviewing the racing form. As we exited the train directly onto the platform at Kempton Park, Joann lost sight of me for a second. She reached around and grabbed the first tall man she saw, thinking it was me. It turned out to be our compartment companion, Cyril Lark. Cyril was a high-level civil servant in the ministry of aviation and could be Hollywood typecasted as a distinguished British citizen. While surprised by Joann accosting him, he was unfazed, and we soon laughed and started a friendship with him and his son, Alan. He guided us into the track and showed us the ropes as we had no idea of where to go or how to go about the rigors of betting. He pointed out the bookie's enclosure. There we saw separate small stands, each with an easel that had a chalkboard and hanging from it a leather bag where money was placed and taken out.

The odds on each horse were set out on the chalkboard. When you made a bet, the bet was written down by hand on a spreadsheet by an assistant at the stand. You were given a numbered ticket from that bookie for that particular bet. There was nothing on the ticket that indicated the odds or indicated the horse that you bet on, just a number for the bet. It was expected that you would remember the bet, and, of course, the bookies had written it down. They always got it right as their integrity in terms of actually honoring the actual bets was of most importance to them. However, it would be possible to get confused and forget which bookie took your bet. If this was on the last race, they may have closed up shop before you figured it out.

Cyril and I took turns buying each other rounds of drinks. We had a pint of bitter and then switched to whiskeys. By the end of the day, we were quite happily involved in British racing. This was made an even happier occasion by the fact that it seemed that Cyril won virtually every race. My mind's eye still remembers watching the races and seeing some magnificent jumps made by a horse as it moved down the far side of the track. I specifically remember this one horse that gained at every jump by perfect timing, a sound landing, and a sprint in the stretch to victory.

Before the day ended, Cyril invited us to his home the next day for an English Sunday dinner. We exchanged information and agreed to meet at a pub at 1:00 pm, where we would have a drink and then go to his home for Sunday dinner. Cyril and Alan decided to extend their day by going off to the evening dog races. We sent them off, telling them we were looking forward to the next day.

The next morning was Sunday. We had gotten wind of a flea market and decided to take a look at it. Our plans were to get a taxi from the flea market to take us to the pub. It turned out that cabs were impossible to find. We became very anxious that we were not going to be there by the 2:00 pm closing time. We finally found a cab and arrived at the pub about five minutes before 2:00 pm Apparently Cyril had gathered many of his friends at the pub and told them about the young American couple who were coming to Sunday dinner. When we did not show at 1:00, I am sure he became most anxious that he had been stood up and was accordingly embarrassed. When we arrived just before closing, he was so relieved to see us that it doubled his enjoyment in having us come. Having made it by the skin of our teeth, our anxieties were relieved, and we were excited about the day.

I remember learning the British tradition of buying rounds of drinks. I had a pint of bitter, and my wife had a sherry. Soon I noticed there were two sherries lined up in front of my wife and two pints in front of me. She dutifully drank them; I finished my pints, and we went off to Cyril's home.

His wife had prepared a traditional British Sunday dinner. It was roast beef with Yorkshire pudding and all the trimmings. It was such a treat to not only have wonderful food but to have it in a setting that was ordinarily inaccessible to a tourist—especially a young couple. Before the meal was over, we were making speeches to each other—he referred to us as "colonials" and I referred to England as the "mother country." After the meal and a brandy and extended toasts, Cyril announced it was opening time at the pub. We went back to the local pub to have another round or two of drinks before we returned to our hotel, the Ruebens, near Buckingham Palace. That day blossomed into a friendship, and for many years on our trips to London, we always had a meal with Cyril and his family. His daughter married a

Canadian and eventually immigrated to Canada. She, on one occasion, visited us at our farm in Vermont.

On one of our trips, we took Cyril and Alan out for dinner. I made a reservation at Veeraswamy's. Veeraswamy's was an Indian Restaurant on Regent Street in London. It was a high-class establishment. This was at a time when there were not the number of good Indian restaurants in London that one finds today. As far as we knew it, was the only Indian Restaurant.

We were greeted at the door by a doorman dressed in traditional Indian robes and a turban. In the downstairs lobby, there was a tiger skin on the wall. The restaurant was on the second floor, and we were escorted to a spacious table. It was then I learned that Cyril did not like Indian food. Roast beef, lamb, potatoes, and peas, and maybe an occasional Dover sole was his standard. Fortunately, the restaurant was aware that occasionally a person would want something other than Indian food and they had something on the menu to accommodate him. I, on the other hand, was anxious to try whatever there was to offer. The thing I remember most about the meal was the soup, rasam. It was so spicy that I immediately got the hiccups, tears streaming from my eyes, and sweating on my forehead. My wife looked at me and said, "Are you okay?" and I said, "This is the most delicious thing I have ever tasted." I meant it.

Unfortunately, Cyril and his wife divorced. He remarried a woman who was a childhood friend, and they moved out of London in retirement to Dartmoor. Our friendship continued, and on one visit we ventured out to his home and he took us to a football game between Plymouth and Argyle. It is the one and only premier football game I have ever seen in person, though I have watched a lot of games on TV. In the course of that visit, we visited several pubs and never seemed to run out of conversation.

CHAPTER 7

Sharing with Friends

The first of many meals shared through a friendship occurred on West 56th Street in New York in the mid-1960s. As a young lawyer trying to build a practice, I joined most any organization that would take me. I became a Mason, then a Shriner, and then a member of the Shriners Drum and Bugle Corps. I had never played a bugle before, but as a high school student I had wrestled with a bassoon and had some idea of making music in a group. I learned enough about the bugle that my fellow members could tolerate me.

The National Shriners convention was being held in New York City, and our bugle corps was to march in a parade at Shea Stadium—the then home of the New York Mets. All around midtown, New York, one could spot the red Fez, the official headgear of the Shriners since 1872, all carrying the names of various Shriner temples across the country. I was alone for lunch on the day that we were scheduled to head to Shea Stadium. Walking down East 56th Street, I spied a small French bistro called "Steak Pommes Frites" and decided to give it a try. I was sporting my fez, which I continued to wear even after being seated at a small table with my back against a wall, looking out over the whole restaurant. I started my meal with a martini and then ordered the featured steak pommes frites. I added a small carafe of red wine and was thoroughly enjoying myself.

It was at this point that the proprietor—a young man in his late twenties—stopped at my table and asked if he could sit down in the extra chair. I welcomed his company. His name was Alex Conte. His mother was one of two partners who owned the restaurant, and he was the manager. In visiting, we learned that we both liked fishing, and I told him about my home in Vermont with its trout stream. As I finished lunch, we made plans to meet again sometime in the future, and I extended an invitation for him to visit Vermont. Our friendship blossomed over the years and resulted in many good meals—both in my home in Vermont and at Steak Pommes Frites in New York. Years later, he told me that he joined me that day because he wondered how a young man wearing a crazy-looking fez could have a luncheon by himself and obviously enjoy it thoroughly.

Alex made his first trip to Vermont in September after our conversation in New York. Remembering my invitation, he looked me up. It was a nice fall day actually, and he caught up with me and some friends on the Middlebury College Golf Course (this was before I learned that if I didn't play golf I could get much more done). We had just a couple holes to go, and he walked along with us. As we came to the 18th hole, we discovered a fairy ring of pink bottom mushrooms. We scrounged a bag and picked about a peck of these wonderful mushrooms. Pink bottoms, for some reason, tend to grow in a fairy circle on open grass. They are a gill mushroom, and their gills are pink in color, and they are closely related to the commercial mushrooms that dominate the shelves of our supermarkets.

As we finished, I insisted we return to the farm for dinner and drinks; I had not expected him, so there was no planned dinner. Luckily, I had a good summer trout fishing, and I was able to retrieve about eighteen small brook trout from the freezer. He took over the cooking, and I became his sous chef for the night. We had a feast of Vermont's natural bounty with the wild trout and the wild mushrooms. The libations, though distilled from nature, were not from Vermont.

I remember sharing another meal with him because of the situation that brought it about. As a young lawyer, I not only joined organizations, but I tried various business ventures. One of these was with a partner, and together we opened up a mobile home sales lot. We were selling Detroiter Mobile Homes, and my partner, a better salesman than a businessman, generated sufficient sales to obtain an invitation to a suppliers retreat; a week in the Bahamas, with all expenses picked up by Detroiter, our main source of mobile homes. Another Vermont dealer, Roger Lussier, with two of his friends, joined the excursion.

On the way back from the Bahamas, the first leg of the flight was late getting into Philadelphia and we missed our connection to Vermont. U.S. Air figured out that if they got us and the Lussier party to Kennedy airport in New York City, we could catch the last plane that night to Burlington. They arranged for a limousine to drive us from Philadelphia to Kennedy Airport. Unfortunately, we did not make that plane either. Stuck in the airport at Kennedy, we found a hotel in the immediate vicinity, and booked a room with plans to catch the next flight in the morning. It was past 10:00 pm, when I called Alex at Steak Pommes Frites, and after an enthusiastic greeting, I asked, "When do you close?" His response was, "For you, I never close." We got to our hotel as quickly as possible and grabbed taxis into downtown Manhattan, arriving at Steak Pommes Frites shortly after 11:00 pm. The restaurant was closed to the public, but he kept it open for us and kept a chef on to make our dinner. I remember the full treatment of martinis, escargot, steak pommes frites along with espresso coffee and a brandy. When I asked for the check, he said he couldn't completely comp me the meal because it was his mother's business, but he was just going to charge me the cost of the food. The bill was reduced by about two-thirds of what the going rate would be.

During the course of the meal, two local policemen on the beat came in for their nightly whiskey "on the house," and we visited with them. In the early hours of the next day, we decided the time had come to go back to our hotel near Kennedy Airport. We suggested to Alex that he call cabs for the eight of us. Alex said that was not going to happen—that he and a friend who was still at the restaurant were going to drive us to the hotel themselves. And so, they did.

Roger Lussier, the president of the Lyndonville Savings Bank, a successful cattle dealer and entrepreneur in the Northeast Kingdom of Vermont, was truly amazed that I was able to arrange such a function and make a special night out of unexpected airline delays. As an aside, I represented Roger some years later in a federal criminal trial, where after three days of deliberations, the jury found him guilty on several counts and he was sentenced to jail. He subsequently sued me for malpractice, but this was after he had fired us and hired F. Lee Bailey to take his appeal. F. Lee Bailey's firm completely screwed up the appeal, which we believe we would have won as the legal position we took was later adopted by the Second Circuit. But in any case, I was joined as a Defendant with F. Lee Bailey in a malpractice suit. The case against our firm was eventually dismissed, and the case against F. Lee Bailey went to the jury, resulting in a verdict in excess of $400,000.

It gave me great pleasure to show off to a bank president how a young country lawyer from Middlebury could have connections to keep a quality New York City restaurant open to accommodate us on the shortest of notices.

I recall another incident with Lussier whose original trade was as a cattle dealer. Lussier was trying to repossess about twenty Holstein heifers from a bankruptcy estate. I had been appointed as trustee for the bankruptcy, and if he succeeded in repossessing all twenty cows, there would be nothing left for the trustee and I would not get paid. At that time, Vermont had not adopted the Uniform Commercial Code and we were still using a chattel mortgage form, which required the listing of each cow by its ear tag number. Somehow, Roger indicated that he could only account for eighteen of the twenty cows' ear tag numbers, leaving two to be sold and enough proceeds to pay me as the trustee. I still have not ever found out why he couldn't find all twenty cows' ear tag numbers, but I believe he was looking out for himself by looking after me.

In the early 1960s, I met a young Vermonter from the Rutland area, Robert Van Beever. He was much involved in Killington's development and was a topflight skier. He had been selected by the local newspaper as the Young Businessman of the Year. Shortly thereafter, he broke both of his legs skiing and that ended his skiing career. He was married and had three young boys.

We decided to try many ventures together, including trying to set up a distribution of Vermont photographs as picture postcards. We never did get it off the ground. However, our friendship continued even when he went to New York City to work for *Golf Digest* magazine. He was a man of many talents. I have one of his oil paintings of a Vermont river scene hanging in our office. He also wrote a paperback novel called *The Bamboo Saucer*, which involved the landing of a spacecraft of Chinese origin in the Middlebury area and used a cigar-smoking young State's Attorney as a protagonist in the novel. It was published, and I do not know how many copies were sold, but it certainly did not make *The New York Times* bestseller list.

Bob told me that he and his wife had separated, and he was in love with a woman in New York City. She had an apartment in Greenwich Village, and he was living with her at the time. I had a conversation with him and explained to him that no way was he going to be able to afford a divorce, which would require him to support his three children and an ex-wife. I suggested that he should reconcile with his wife, forget the woman in New York, and use his many talents to become a success. He said I was probably right, but he wanted me to meet his new love.

I was staying with my parents in Queens, and I agreed to take the subway into New York and have dinner with him and his lady friend at her apartment in the village.

There were two images in my mind—one being a second-rate apartment populated by what in those days we called bohemians. I expected that most likely my visit would be to a disorganized, small, and somewhat dingy apartment. The other image I had was of a sophisticated apartment with polished floors occupied by a well-coiffured woman in beautiful surroundings.

When I arrived, I was met at the door by Bob and his lady friend, who had a martini in her hand that she immediately gave to me. She was dressed in a flowing Japanese kimono and was both gorgeous and gracious. We had a carefully prepared and delicious dinner. The conversation was stimulating, and my friend's lady was absolutely delightful. As I left, he insisted upon walking with me to the subway entrance. On the way, he asked me what I thought. Thinking of the advice I gave him about going back to his wife and abandoning this woman, my only response was, "Bob, I think you've got a problem." Within the year, he had gotten a divorce and had married his new love, and they had moved to Westport, Connecticut.

He invited me to come down and visit him in Westport, where he was running a liquor store. I drove down Route 7 from my home in Salisbury. On the way, when I got to Ridgefield, Connecticut, I saw a roadside stand that had a sign out for cut flowers. I stopped to buy some flowers for my hostess. I was greeted by the proprietor of the roadside stand—a man by the name of Eric Lawaetz. He took me out to his beautiful gardens where he proceeded to cut flowers. It turned out he was Danish, and, while pleasant, a bit gruff. He complained how dry the summer had been, and I said it may have been dry, but my home area in Vermont was probably even drier. He asked me where I lived, and I told him in Salisbury, Vermont—near Middlebury. He then told me that he had a hundred acres of land in Shoreham, Vermont— just a few miles away from Middlebury. I then introduced myself as Peter Langrock, and he said, "Oh, your father must be the State's Attorney," and I said, "No, that's me." This surprised him. It also turned out I had represented him in the title work that was required when he purchased the Shoreham property. Our conversation extended and we got into the subject of hunting.

He told me that he was an avid hunter. I later learned he had been raised in Denmark where his father managed an estate and acted as gamekeeper. He had immigrated to the United States at the age of nineteen after a dispute with his father, who blamed Europe's depression after World War I on him. He had decided to strike out on his own.

In our conversation, he told me that each year he went to James Bay and hunted geese with the Cree Indians and asked if I would be interested in joining him sometime. I said it sounded like fun and I certainly would be interested. The following winter, he stopped by my office and renewed the question of whether I would like to go to James Bay with him the following fall. I said I would, and he agreed to try to make the arrangements. A few days later, he called and apologized. He said he tried to get a reservation for me to join him, but that they were completely booked. I thought nothing of it and said, "Well, maybe some other time." We had a nice conversation, and each went our own way. In late September, I received a call, and it was

Eric. He said, "I know it is impossible, but I thought I had a responsibility to ask you. I just got a call from the person running the James Bay camp, and he said they just had a cancellation and now had an opening." He said he was sure it would be impossible for me to make plans on such short notice as he would be leaving in three days, but he thought it was his duty to ask me. I replied, "Give me a few hours, and let me see what I can do to clear my schedule."

I called him back within the hour, and it was agreed that we would go together. He was to come to Salisbury, spend the night, and we would drive from there to Timmins, Ontario. From there, we would fly north to James Bay for the hunt with the Crees. This was the beginning of a long and lasting friendship. It was a two-day driving trip. On the way up, we stopped in Ottawa where we found a restaurant and had a Steak Diane accompanied by a decent bottle of a French claret. We continued on to North Bay where we spent the night, and the next day we made it on to Timmins.

At Timmins, we stayed at the Excelsior Hotel. In my room, I discovered their version of a fire escape. It was a rope tied to the radiator next to the window with knots in it that one could use to repel out the window in case of a fire. This was Timmins before it had really caught on economically. It was just at the beginning of the Gulf Sulfur Mine near Timmins. The next day, with our guns and duffle bag, we arrived at the airport to be loaded on to a converted PBY—the famous gray goose of World War II—the flying boat. It took off on land; the inside had not been changed very much from its military days.

The landing was a different matter. There was no airport at the small settlement at the mouth of the Albany River, which was the home of the Crees in the area. We landed with the plane's belly connecting with the Albany River, stabilized by a small pontoon hanging from each wing. There we were greeted by several Hudson Bay canoes manned by Cree men who unloaded our baggage into the canoes then unloaded us and took us to the camp on an island at the river mouth.

Our camp basically was divided in two parts, with a breezeway in between. At the north was the living space provided for Anna, who was the camp cook and major force at the camp. She was a lovely person who had long experience in cooking in logging camps throughout the north and left no doubt that she was the boss. She had a wood cook stove and could turn out marvelous pies and also cooked the best goose I have ever eaten. The south building was the dormitory, with bunk beds, a table, and a pack of cards. There were windows on the inside and a screen on the outside. We were able to bring beer we had brought with us, Labattes Cinquante, and put it in between the screen and the windows to keep it cold.

Our first day of shooting proved that I was not as good a shot as I thought I was, and while we got a couple of geese, we did not reach our limit of five each. The other hunters in the camp were more successful, and they were bragging about the fact that they all had limited out.

Embedded in the camp was a Royal Canadian Mounted Police Officer who was there to ensure that the laws relating to the taking of geese were strictly followed. He was a young corporal full of stories—some of which I can't repeat here. As Eric and I were both liberals, we were mindful of the fact that First Americans were not treated as well as they should have been by the Canadian Government. Anna was also a liberal, and she found our attitudes welcome as compared to the much more conservative and sometimes offensive conservatism that many of the hunters espoused. We had a wonderful time, and our shooting improved, and we went home with the ten geese and some ducks that were the maximum we were allowed to bring back to the United States. The Cree women plucked and dressed all the birds, saving the down from the geese to be sold for use by the manufacturers of goose down-filled parkas. On our return to Timmins, the geese were all packed in a special cardboard box designed to keep each goose protected and a supply of dry ice was available so that we could get them home in good condition.

I had such a good time that when we made our reservations for the next year, I suggested that I would like some of my friends to experience it as well. Eric agreed with a bit of hesitation. On the following trip, we proceeded along the same lines, only with two cars full of my hunting friends from Vermont, as well as Eric. During that trip, I played host to these people and spent a lot of time making sure that they had a good time. After the hunt and the return to Vermont, we dropped everybody off. It was just Eric and myself going back to the home farm, when I turned to him and I said, "Eric, I think it was more fun when just the two of us went." He replied, "I could have told you so, but I thought you had to learn for yourself."

We continued going each fall for a period of sixteen years—sometimes with others and sometimes by ourselves. During the course of our travels, we discovered that between North Bay and Timmins there was a Danish restaurant. That became our stopover for lunch. I would drive until we got there, and then I would partake of some wonderful Danish dishes, but the thing I remember most was the Aquavit, which flowed freely. I turned over the rest of the drive to Timmins to someone else.

The history of the Crees at Fort Albany is an interesting one. Two groups of missionaries came to try to convert the Crees to Christianity. One was Roman Catholic, and the other was Anglican. This resulted in the tribe dividing itself and eventually forming two separate settlements. There is little interchange between them and little intermarriage. So much for the good done by competing Christian missionaries.

Our guide through all those seasons was Claudius Huey, a strong, independent individual with a good sense of humor. A full-page picture of him is in the October 1978 *National Geographic Magazine*. Sixteen years of hunting with the Crees—and especially with Claudius—resulted in many stories.

One of the things that happened over the sixteen years was that we saw the transition of the Indian settlement moving from a self-sustaining society to a welfare-dependent society. Where once the winter food supply was based upon killing a moose and stocking up several hundred geese, it was replaced by white bread and canned goods available at the Hudson Bay Store located at the permanent Cree Anglican settlement. This settlement consisted of various simple but efficient houses and about a mile and a half of roadway. The fact that it was only a mile and a half of roadway did not prevent the presence of a police cruiser that patrolled with a fully uniformed police officer.

Part of the trip involved going to an outpost, which was about twenty miles north up the bay. There we stayed overnight at a large tent set on a wooden platform. The geese, ducks, and snipe were plentiful. At times you could see a flock of 10,000 geese undulating along the horizon, setting down and picking up.

On one occasion, someone brought some marijuana. Before lighting up a joint, paranoia took over and we carefully looked out on the horizon to see if there were any mounties looking for us across the vast expanses of flat land comprising the shore of James Bay.

One time we had a very successful duck hunting day and left the ducks in the front of our canoe. The next morning, the ducks were missing. An investigation discovered that a skunk had removed all the ducks and hid them under the tent platform. The guides—very carefully, with a long stick—shooed the skunk away and retrieved the ducks.

For what turned out to be our last trip, I had purchased a pair of stocking waders. These were made of very flexible rubber and had a sock bottom made of that same rubber. You wore sneakers over them, and they were much more comfortable for the long walks one took going to the blinds and for crouching down when the geese were being drawn into the decoys. For decoys, we initially used some white plastic bags tied to some brush. As we shot the geese, we retrieved them, and then propped them up with a stick to look like a flock set down near the blinds.

By this trip, the discipline that we initially saw in running the camp had deteriorated. The village had graduated to snowmobiles, and the children were more adventurous and devious. One night, I hung my waders in the breezeway between the north and the south parts of the camp. In the morning, when I came out to put on my waders, my feet went right through. Much to my surprise the bottom half of both legs had been cut off. The waders were useless. That day, walking around the camp, I saw that each of the youngsters had brand-new slingshots using the rubber from my boots. We stopped our annual trip when the Canadian government turned over the franchise of the hunting camp to the Crees and the organization that had organized the hunt fell apart.

The old PBYs that we originally flew and landed in the river became obsolete when a small airfield had been built, which accommodated DC3s from Timmins to the camp.

When we were hunting, Claudius thought it great fun to tell me that a flock of geese were coming and to crouch down, putting my head down, saying he would tell me when to stand and shoot. We could hear the geese getting closer, and all of a sudden Claudius would say, "Shoot, shoot." As I stood, the geese would sometimes be a mile high, but in the excitement I would still fire my gun with no chance of bringing a bird down. Claudius enjoyed that joke, and we enjoyed his laugh.

One time when I arrived on the DC3, Claudius was waiting, and as I got out, he shouted, "Pete, shoot, shoot," much to the amusement of all there who knew me from past years.

Another adventure occurred on our return trip to Timmons. The PBYs had a usual airspeed of approximately 120 knots. This particular day we were running into a head wind of about sixty knots, thus, our ground speed was something in the order of sixty knots. We were running low on fuel. We knew we could make an emergency landing most anywhere, as there was water all over the area. However, we diverted and ended up in a small airport, where we were able to refuel and get back to Timmins in reasonable time.

Claudius was an amazing shot. One day we had limited out and were returning from the blind toward the canoe, crossing through willows. I handed my gun to Claudius and told him to shoot some birds for his own use. Soon, a flock of snow geese passed over the willows which hid us. I was surprised that he didn't shoot right away. I soon found out why—he was waiting for two birds to cross in flight so that he could get them both with one shot. No wasting of expensive ammunition by Claudius.

CHAPTER 8

Good Meals, Good Friends

My mentor in law school was Soia Mentschikoff. She was married to Karl Llewellyn. They were both among the truly great law teachers of the 20th century. I thought highly of them and remember being invited to their home in Hyde Park for dinner along with one other student. It was an experience that I still cherish to this day. Karl Llewellyn favored Manhattans, and while I don't remember what we had for dinner, I do remember enjoying a Manhattan at his home.

It was Soia who played a significant role in giving me advice at critical times in my life. The first time was when I was participating in a moot court at the law school. Soia was one of three judges who heard our arguments. After it was over, she looked at me. "I didn't think much of your brief, but you might make a decent jury lawyer someday." My career was set in that direction from there on.

The second time she helped me make a decision was perhaps even more important. I had taken a course in patent law from then Dean Edward Levy, later U.S. Attorney General under President Gerald Ford. Each week, we were required to do a paper from a list of topics that he provided. The actual seminar was held in his rather small office and sometimes several of us would have to remain standing. On one occasion, I chose plant patents as a topic from his list. This was in 1958. Crick and Watson had released their papers on DNA in 1953, and I was fortunate enough to have read them in their original form while I was at the college. Plant patents deal with asexual reproduction with no change of gene structure, as opposed to sexual reproduction where DNA deals with the joining of different genes. Dean Levy, who is known as the best Attorney General the United States has ever had, was both brilliant and had broad-ranged interests. However, in responding to my paper, it was obvious from his margin notes that he had not kept current on the progress in the DNA field made by Crick and Watson. I rewrote the paper responding to his notes and submitted it to the Journal of Patent Office Society, and they published it: "Biological Necessities in Infringement Suits." I came back to my senior year in law school—not as a member of The Law Review but with a published article in a reputable legal journal. As a result of that, he thought I might be of sufficient ability to handle a court of appeals clerkship. He approached me and asked if I would be interested in clerking for Judge Pope, the Chief Judge of the Ninth Circuit Court of Appeals in San Francisco. I do not know whether I would have gotten the job, but I expect with his recommendation I would have had a good chance to get it.

Wandering through the stacks, I stopped by the open door to Soia's office. She asked me if something was bothering me. I went into her office and told her I was trying to make up my mind whether I should apply for a clerkship with Judge Pope or whether I should go back home and run for State's Attorney—back home being in Middlebury. She looked at me and said simply, "Where do you want to live eventually?" I said, "Vermont." She responded, "What in the hell are you talking about going to San Francisco for?" I walked out, my mind made up, and came back to Vermont—a decision

I have never regretted. The interesting thing is, I am sure that every other member of the faculty would have advised me to do just the opposite. They would have advised that the clerkship would be a great opportunity and that I could always go back to Vermont afterward. They would have been wrong. I am sure I would have been seduced by a San Francisco law firm, and if I had been successful, at retirement, I could have reached the financial point where I could afford to live like I have for the last sixty years.

Some years later, after being a colleague of Soia's in the Uniform Law Conference, I was invited to become a member of the visiting committee at the University of Miami Law School where she was the dean. I accepted and found myself in the company of such illustrious persons as former Attorney Generals Levy, Katzenbach (another of my professors), and Judge Wisdom. There was also a lawyer there who was a student of Soia's from Dallas. His name was Jim Donohoe. He stood several inches over six feet and was big not only in stature but in voice. We soon had a discussion and discovered we were both bird hunters. That resulted in us quickly playing the game of "my bird dog is better than your bird dog." Starting with that discussion we became close friends and broke bread on many trips hunting quail in, West Texas, prairie chickens in South Dakota, pheasants in Nebraska, snow geese and ducks in northern Ontario, and ruffed grouse in Vermont.

On a visit to his home in Dallas, I saw that Jim had a collection of *National Geographic Magazines*. I pulled out the 1978 October magazine, which had a full-page picture of Claudius Huey, a Cree Indian from Fort Albany on James Bay at the southern tip of Hudson Bay. As mentioned, Claudius had been my hunting guide in previous years. The picture whetted Jim's appetite, and the next fall we ended up at the mouth of the Albany River.

In an outpost about twenty miles from the main camp at the mouth of the Albany River, we hunted snow geese, blue geese, ducks, and Wilson's snipe. While sitting in a blind, he relayed to me a story about his early years working at a firm in Dallas. He had been assigned by a senior partner to deal with a very difficult client in a complicated real estate closing. The partner apparently really did not want to deal with the client himself and was happy to have the responsibility fall on Jim. Apparently, the closing went well and the partner was so pleased with Jim's performance that he invited him to The Dallas Club for a drink. At The Dallas Club, they had a drink together before the partner had to leave. On leaving, he said to Jim, "You stay here and have whatever you want to drink and eat, and the bill will come to me." Jim took advantage of the situation. About two weeks later, he received a message to report to the partner. As he walked into the office, the partner had the bill from the club in front of him. He looked at Jim and said, "Thirteen martinis?" Jim told me he has no recollection of how he got home that night.

Many times in Texas we shared wonderful Texas BBQ. We did this both in rural Texas and in some of Dallas' favorite BBQ haunts. I have never had better BBQ anywhere.

Of the many occasions we shared libations, I remember best what occurred one night when we were coming down the west shore of James Bay from an outpost north of the main camp in a Hudson Bay canoe. Claudius was at the motor as we headed south. Jim and I were crouched facing north at the front of the canoe under a canvas to keep the spray off our backs while we shared a bottle of Canadian Club. It was a brilliant night, and the northern sky was full with a display of northern lights that I have never seen equaled at any time. The two of us passed the bottle back and forth and enjoyed the greatest light show on earth.

Tony Turner was an Englishman who thought he was Welsh. He spoke Welsh, thought Welsh, and tried to regulate his English birth to a minor role. He also thought of himself as an old-fashioned farmer. By old-fashioned, I mean he basically kept a flock of sheep, raised pigs, chickens, and an occasional calf. He had a special liking for a breed of sheep called "Clun Forest." These are medium-sized sheep with high-quality spinning wool and a nice, European, lean carcass.

Tony decided he would immigrate to the United States and bring with him some "cluns." Before sheep can enter the United States, they have to undergo a six-year quarantine. This is done to prevent the spread of scrapie, a sheep disease, in the United States. He handled this by moving to Canada, keeping his sheep there, and finally, after the six-year quarantine was over, moved them to Shoreham, Vermont. During this time, his wife continued her teaching job in Wales and was able to keep the family homestead going.

Tony was a lover of the theater and an accomplished storyteller. He participated in local community theater and started his own radio show on Saturday morning on our local AM station WFAD. Middlebury was proud to have its own station, and this was before the rise of National Public Radio. His show was called "Speaking From the Hills," and he had many guests to the show. He used it as a bully pulpit to complain about the introduction of the metric system, saying it was a horror and that we should stick to the traditional measures of ounces, inches, feet, yards, and miles.

In order to get back across the pond to visit his home and his wife, he took people on sheep tours of England and Wales. Joann was just getting interested in sheep, and she signed up for one of Tony's tours. The bane and beauty of Tony's tours were that they were all inclusive, and whenever he could scrounge lodgings or a meal from friends and acquaintances on the other side of the Atlantic, he did so. This included his mom's home in northern Wales. Besides viewing sheep and visiting several farms, the tour group, small—only five—also visited wonderful sites such as Bodnant

Gardens. Joann suggested that the group take Tony's mom out to lunch as a thank you for putting up with Tony's tour crowd and steering them towards Bodnant. They chose the Gwydyr Inn in Betws Y Coed for the occasion. The choice of this inn resulted in Joann discovering Violet Smith, the proprietor from whom she learned that the hotel had fishing rights for salmon in the Conway River. One could book in at the hotel and obtain a right to fish a stretch of the Conway. Fishing rights in Europe are privately owned and not open to the public. Joann brought a brochure home, and the next spring, Joann, myself, and our friends, Bill and Charmain Rule, took off for a trip for two weeks in the U.K., including a week in north Wales to fish salmon and enjoy the countryside and its pubs.

At the Gwydyr, among other guests, was a Mrs. Perrin and her thirty-year-old son who had come from Worcestershire for their yearly visit to fish the Conway. For the first three days of our adventure, I flailed the Conway with all the flies that I had in my tackle box and saw the occasional leaping salmon but had no success whatsoever in hooking one. On the fourth day, I watched Perrin fish a pool along the stretch of river that I was scheduled to have for the next day. I carefully watched his technique, aware that each night in the previous three days he had brought home some very nice salmon—some over ten pounds. In talking with him, he claimed that he had caught them on a size No. 4 blue charm fly. My No. 4 blue charm had not produced any results. I learned that evening, much to my surprise, that he actually sold locally the fish that he caught. This was something I had not encountered with sports fishermen previously. On the fifth day, I approached this new stretch of the river with my gilly, Railroad Bob. (Most of his life, Railroad Bob had worked on maintaining a small passenger station on the railroad that ran through the Conway Valley.) We went to the particular pool I had seen Perrin fishing and started fishing the way he did—working my way down the north side of the pool. Railroad Bob turned to me and said, "What are you doing?" "I'm fishing just like Mr. Perrin did yesterday," I said, thinking about his success. He looked at me. "You don't believe him, do you? He was decoying you. He doesn't use flies; he uses shrimp. Come here, let me put a shrimp on for you." I did, and within a few minutes I had hooked onto a nice salmon. After landing it, it turned out to be a seven-pound hen fish.

I was quite pleased with it, and when I returned to Gwydyr, I showed it to Mrs. Perrin. Her comment was, "Oh, that's a nice little fish." It may have been little in her eyes, but to me it was an accomplishment having finally caught a salmon in the Conway. I talked to Violet Smith and told her that I would like the chef to prepare the fish for our party and for the other guests in the hotel. That evening we all had a course of fresh salmon from the Conway, courtesy of myself, the chef, and a small gratuity that was passed to the chef. Actually, there was even enough left over so that the next day some was served as a cold appetizer.

Previous to the lunch, I had told my wife about my being decoyed by Perrin and that I thought he was an unmitigated bastard. She thought my evaluation was a little harsh, but she heard what I said. At lunch that day, he came over to me and said, "I see you caught a nice little salmon. It was very kind of you to share that with everyone; too bad they didn't prepare it better." As he walked away, my wife turned to me and said, "He is an unmitigated bastard."

That fishing expedition led into another major friendship in my life. I had been involved for many years raising and racing trotting horses. I held a full driver's license and would race both at the Saratoga Harness Track and at fairs throughout the Northeast. I don't claim to be a great driver, but I managed to have a fair number of wins. I was talking about harness racing with Railroad Bob when he told me that in the next town over, Llangernyw, there was a farmer by the name of Alun Jones, who trained harness horses. He told me how to get to his farm, and the next day, as we departed Betws Y Coed to head north on the rest of our vacation, we made a short detour to look up Alun Jones. After traveling between high hedge fences on single-laned roads, we eventually found his farm and knocked at the door. A young woman in a bathrobe with her hair in a towel fresh from the shower opened the door and asked if she could help us. I explained to her that I was from the United States and interested in harness horses. It was Alun's daughter, and she told us her father was off to Applebee in the north of England—almost to the Scottish border—for a race meet that was being held there. After a short and friendly discussion, we retraced down the one-lane road until we hit a main highway where my car seemed, on its own, to keep making turns towards Applebee. We arrived at Applebee and found lodgings and then went to the site of the race meet. Much to my surprise, it was not a regular track but a large field with horse vans scattered through a large area. The races were conducted over the field with the course marked by white stakes. There was a small hill where the spectators watched the races and where there was an enclosure where the bookies had set up their stands. By asking around, we finally found Alun Jones and I introduced myself to him. He was busy that day getting ready for the final race. He won the heat, making his horse the champion of the meet. I came back to see him after the race was over, and we had the chance to have a more relaxed visit. At that time, I told him that if he was ever in the United States, I would be happy to show him around the tracks in the northeast. I gave him my card and went on my way.

Sometime later I received a letter from him, and it was decided that he would take me up on my offer and visit us over Thanksgiving weekend.

Alun Jones was quite a man. He was born on a farm on the side of the Snowdon Mountain in west Wales. As a young man, he daily traveled twenty-five miles, each way by horseback, to attend to his flock that were at Llangenyw. He had been a sparring partner with Randy Turpin, a world middleweight champion, and was also the hand-shearing champion for all of Wales. These accomplishments were nothing compared to his ability to down pint and after pint and then go into something which was less in quantity but certainly not less strong.

I arranged to pick up Alun at the airport and take him to our farm, which is about an hour drive south of Burlington. About half-way down, I voiced that in another twenty minutes we would be at home and we would be able to have a libation. I heard an audible sigh. He later told me that as they arrived in Burlington, he turned to Mary, his wife, and said, "What if they're teetotalers?" Thankfully for both of us, we weren't.

Thanksgiving dinner went well with the turkey, cranberry sauce, and traditional New England side dishes. Our drinks matched the quality of the food, and the conversations were convivial. Sometime after dinner, both Alun and I were napping sitting up-right in our chairs in the living room. Alun, who is bald, presented a temptation, and Mary and my daughter, Katie, decorated the top of his head with a magic marker. When he awoke, he couldn't figure what everybody was laughing at until he looked in the mirror.

The day after Thanksgiving is celebrated as a holiday in our office, and while we had things to do during the day, we had not made any specific plans for Friday night. It occurred to me that BlueBonnets Racetrack in Montreal, the home to some of Canada's best harness horses, would be open that night. We decided to drive to Montreal. It's about a two-and-a-half hour drive, so I called the Queen Elizabeth Hotel and made reservations for us for the night. We arrived at the track in time for the first race. When we were looking over the program, Alun was surprised that a horse that he had owned and raced in Wales and eventually was sold for export to Canada was on the program that night. Of course, we backed this horse. Alun, perhaps as a result of the good feelings that in part may have been due to the drinking and eating that weekend, decided to put a reasonably hefty bet on the horse. Coming into the top of the stretch, the horse made a move to the outside and caught the lead horse just before the finish line. We both immediately got up from the table and went down towards the winner's circle and explained to the photographer that we wanted a picture with the winning horse for Alun to take back to Wales. We then celebrated the win with a Havana cigar (legal in Canada) and a large brandy.

The next spring on Bank Holiday in May, I flew to Wales so that I could join Alun and Mary and return to the meet at Applebee. It was a meeting where the horses raced a distance of almost two miles around the same big green field, which had recently been inhabited by flocks of sheep. Alun had a good day, but he was not the champion for a second time running. It was on that trip that it was decided that their daughter, Megan, who was fifteen, would come to visit us for the summer

Joann and I, together with our daughter, ended up picking up Megan in early summer at Logan Airport in Boston. We stayed at a hotel in Boston that night. For dinner, we went to a restaurant for a New England shore dinner with lobster, steamers, and a full panoply of accompanying dishes. Megan, who had never eaten a Maine lobster, was nonplussed, dug into it, and thoroughly enjoyed it. The next day we drove back to the farm in Vermont. Along the way, much of the land is forested. The land may once have been fields but now most of New England is covered in forested land. Megan looked out at those trees and said to us, "Look at all this wasted land." This was a response to her view of Wales, where virtually all the land was meadows with only small patches of woods standing here and there. She spent a wonderful summer with us and became friends with my daughter, Katie, and that friendship exists to this day. For many years, I tried to take a week at the end of May for the Bank Holiday weekend to go to Applebee—sometimes by myself and sometimes with Joann.

On one occasion, Joann and I were staying at a small hotel in Applebee, and like true Vermonters, we like to leave a window open to let the night air in. We were in the back of the hotel on the ground floor. About 2:00 am, something startled me, and I woke up to see a hand reaching through the window. I sat upright and grunted something, and the hand moved out rapidly, and as I went to the window, I could see somebody hurdling across the various fences between the back of the hotel where we were staying and the roadway. Needless to say, we were a bit shaken by this event and turned on the TV for company to find that the only thing we could get was a movie in Swahili with English subtitles. The next morning, we reported the incident to the front desk and the constables were called. We gave them a statement, and they indicated that they thought they knew who it was and suggested that he was trying to break into the hotel to get to the bar for some free liquor. We never heard any more about the incident.

In one of the early visits to the Jones, I found that Megan was enamored of pickled onions and a certain mint. I accompanied Mary on a shopping trip to a store—something like a small Costco—and bought a gallon jar of pickled onions and a gallon jar of the mints for Megan's enjoyment. She was pleasantly shocked at the size of the gift, and I was assured that none of them went to waste. I must confess I am also a fan of England's pickled onions, and the mints aren't bad either.

Our families' relationships blossomed over the years. Alun decided to bring back to Wales a stallion named "Speedy Sicily" that I owned. Horse transport was more reasonable in those days, and Alun got him back to Wales by riding with the horse in the cargo space for around $2,500. The horse survived the trip, and I received my share of stud fees that about equaled our cost in getting him there. His prodigy, many generations removed, is still racing in Wales.

Alun could not only raise racehorses and raise sheep, but he could sing. He was a friend of Bryn Terfel, one of the world's great opera singers born and raised in a town next to Llangernyw. The singing at pubs in Wales is always delightful. This was a time when there were strict closing hours. Many times, we decided we wanted to continue drinking beyond the legal closing time. This was often accomplished by my registering as an in-house guest at the pub as I would then be allowed to drink behind the sheltered door with my guests after the normal drinking hours. The other alternative was for the landlord to simply close the shades, allowing us to continue in a tone-downed environment. Alun's eye was always kept out for the possibility of a constable interrupting our party. On one occasion, we were drinking at 11:00 pm when closing came, and it was suggested that we continue on at a local farmer's house—some two miles away from the pub. I was deemed to be the designated driver, and I was asked as I went down the road towards the farm how I like to be driving on the wrong side of the road. I responded jokingly that I always drove on the wrong side of the road when I had been drinking.

Over the course of time, our friendship continued, and so much of it was based upon our enjoying meals together, including traditional English breakfasts of fried bacon, eggs, and bread, and occasionally blood sausage. It was also nourished by our enjoying numerous pints as well as good whiskey and occasionally good port.

In the spirit of international agriculture, whenever I visited Applebee, I always brought a quart of maple sugar to Alun as a gift. He always welcomed it enthusiastically, and I thought no more of it. One year, however, while Joann was helping prepare a meal in the farm kitchen, she looked in the pantry and saw there were five quarts of maple syrup carefully stored away that had never been opened. She said nothing, but from thereon my gift when I went to Wales was not maple syrup.

I had a tough choice to make. I was invited to attend a tea in New York City sponsored by ABA's Section of Individual Rights and Responsibilities. The tea was for Ruth Bader Ginsburg who I knew from the days when I chaired the section of Individual Rights and Responsibilities and she was on the council. She had, on one occasion, visited our farm. The same day I was also invited to work as a guest line cook at Quilty's restaurant—a gourmet restaurant in New York whose chef was Katie Sparks, the daughter of my closest friend, Kim Sparks. I opted for the chance to work as a line cook.

My shift started at 3:00 in the afternoon where, after changing into traditional kitchen whites, I started doing prep work. I chopped parsley and filled the poussin—a small fowl—with parsley. I helped break up roasted lobster shells to work towards a lobster sauce.

As opening time came, we were ready to serve the first customers of the evening. I was assigned two tasks. One was to prepare the racks of lamb for grilling. The other was to handle the roasting of the poussin. The kitchen was small and to move around was ballet in action. There was a counter that separated the cooking area from the passageway into the dining room. The waitstaff obtained the meals from the dining room side, and on the cooking side was a gas stove and grill/oven working space. Katie was perched on a stool on the dining room side, where she inspected each dish before it went out into the restaurant. On the cooking side, there were two other line cooks besides the sous chef and myself. There were also two dish and pot washers.

Soon, a waiter came in and said, "Ordering a rack of medium-rare lamb." This put me into action. I took a rack of lamb, which was a double-boned chop that had been carefully trimmed and placed in a small refrigerator under the work counter. I basted it with herbed oil and handed it to the sous chef who did the first grilling. The grill consisted of metal strips going in one direction with a hot flame beneath it. At first the outer edges were seared with one-way strips going parallel to the bones. It was then turned so that the same strips would form a cross pattern across the outside. This took four specific maneuvers to accomplish. Then each side of the rack was charred, first in one direction and then in a cross direction. This required another four maneuvers. The chop was then handed back to me to rest until it was ready to be finished before being served. About twenty minutes later, the same waiter came in and said, "Fire on the rack of lamb." At this point, my job was to place the rack of lamb into a finishing oven that was at 500° for nine minutes. It was also my signal to get some chutney warmed in addition to the finished plate. One of the other line cooks was sautéing spinach in butter. The sous chef took a dish of scalloped potatoes from a warming oven and, using a round cookie cutter, cut out a perfect circular section of the layered potatoes and placed it in the center of a dinner plate. As the lamb came out of the finishing oven, it was handed to the sous chef who cut it in half and arranged the two pieces leaning against the scalloped potatoes. He then took the sautéed spinach from the other line cook and placed it around the base of the potatoes and took the chutney from me and arranged it on the plate. The finished dish was then handed through to Katie to approve before going out to the dining room. This single order had required the attention of three cooks with various responsibilities and the executive chef's approval. I had never focused before on how labor intensive a single dish can be.

If you wish to get high-quality food in a top restaurant, it is always best to go in with a small party. A simple rack of lamb is not something that can be turned out in large numbers and coordinated with different entrees without there being delays caused by the extensive demands on kitchen personnel to make even a single dish. You can imagine the chaos in a kitchen for a party of ten who are all expecting different entrees coming out at the same time. The smaller the number of diners in the party, the less time a dish waits for the other selections before being served.

The shift was especially fun for me as obviously I was not a professional and was only there by the grace of the executive chef who gave me a chance to have the experience. The other people in the kitchen were most kind and made sure that I got a taste of everything that was being prepared on the menu. I did, however, hold up my end of the job and worked hard for several hours. When it was all through, the sous chef sent me out to the dining room: "Now I am going to fix a rack of lamb for you." Not only did he fix the lamb for me, but Katie joined me and opened a bottle of Nuis St. George burgundy. It was a splendid dinner.

The next time Katie came to visit her parents in Vermont, I invited her over for dinner at my house. What does one feed to one of New York's top chefs? I had an answer. A client of mine had been witness to a young moose being hit and killed by a car. He had managed to talk to the game warden at the scene and purchased the moose for a modest sum and took it home to be hung and butchered. In the kindest of gestures, he brought a full tenderloin of the moose to me. I prepared the tenderloin in filets, much like you do a filet mignon of beef, and kept them rare. Moose, in my opinion, is the very best of all meats. It is flavorful, well grained, and tender.

The moose was a complete success at the dinner table. It was a treat that Katie, with all her contacts of purveyors in New York City, could not have duplicated. I suggested to her that when she was back in New York and was questioned about what she was served for meals in the hick country of Vermont, she could simply answer "roadkill." This was not my only roadkill experience.

CHAPTER 9

Courting Joann

In the summer of 1959, I had a job as summer law clerk with Wynn Understood. He kept me busy, but it was a job without pay. In Vermont, you had to serve a six-month clerkship with a member of the bar before you could be admitted to practice, and this was usually an unpaid clerkship. I had to find a place to stay and get three meals a day. I approached the manager of the Middlebury Inn and suggested I would be a good bartender and that I would be happy to work just for room and board. At the Middlebury Inn, there was then a small bar just off the main dining room called the Snow Bowl where there were hand-painted ski murals on the wall highlighting Middlebury College's ski area, the Snow Bowl. He thought about it and, realizing the plight I was in, offered me the job of running the bar at night and at lunch. I was assigned a room at the inn near the kitchen, and I got free meals. The manager later realized this might violate the labor laws, and as the arrangement was actually working out quite well for the inn, I got the usual small salary paid to wait personnel.

At noon every weekday there was a businessmen's luncheon. Between six and twelve people who ran the major businesses in Middlebury would come to the inn for lunch. Sometimes they would be joined by attorneys and sometimes they would order drinks. Occasionally Jack Conley—a great old Irish trial lawyer—would come and start with a martini. His first martini began with a sip from the glass sitting on the table, but by the second sip he was able to lift the glass without shaking and spilling the drink. I remember I could always count on a ten-cent tip from Jack.

I was twenty-one at the time, and, therefore, it was legal for me to serve drinks. For many years I had served as an ad hoc bartender at various events, starting when I was fifteen. I knew a good deal about fixing drinks, but sometimes I could not recall off the top of my head what was required for a particular cocktail.

One evening, a group of students from the summer school came in, which included a rather attractive young woman. She ordered a Cuba libre. I should have known exactly how a Cuba libre was made, but my memory skipped a beat and I had to look in the bar book to be sure. My eye caught a recipe for a Cuba libre "cocktail." It consisted of a shot of rum and an ounce of Coca-Cola, shaken and served with a small slice of lime in a martini glass. I made it according to directions and brought it to the woman at the table. As I approached, she saw what I was serving, and it was obvious to me that it was not what she expected. At that point, an idea appeared like a bubble over my head, and I realized that a Cuba libre was nothing more than a rum and coke. As I sat down the drink I said, "Or did you want one of the tall ones?" She looked relieved and said, "Yes." I took the martini glass back, poured its contents into a regular glass, poured in some more coke and brought it back to her. On arriving at the table, I offered, "I hope this one isn't too strong the way I made it." She tasted it and said it was the best Cuba libre she'd ever had. From there on, I knew whenever she and her friend came in, I had to make it the same way, skipping the martini glass.

Over the Fourth of July weekend of the summer of '59, Joann, my then girlfriend and now my wife for over sixty-five years, had just returned from a year of study in Paris. By way of Washington, D.C., she was coming up to see me before she headed off to be with her parents in San Diego. We had met the previous summer when she was a student at Middlebury College's summer school before heading to Paris for a year studying for her master's degree. She was under an edict as a student in the summer school to speak only French.

She had come to the Waybury Inn with three male fellow students and was sitting at a table near the bar. I arrived with some friends, coming from a sailing club party at Lake Dunmore. The room was filled with students from the various foreign language summer schools and singing broke out in songs in various languages. I decided to join the fun and led a rendition of "Alouette," standing up with exaggerated movements. I learned to do this over many steins of beer at the University of Chicago fraternity parties. I still lead it annually at the Uniform Law Commission's annual meeting "sing along." Everybody joined in, and once it finished, I had an excuse to start a conversation with this attractive young woman whose chair was exactly in back of mine.

My limited knowledge of French allowed us to just barely communicate in public, but I was able to start a conversation in French about having seen the opera Andre Chenier at the Lyric Opera in Chicago. It was the only opera I had ever seen at that point, but I could brag about the cast: Tebaldi, Del Monoco, and Gobbi, the best voices in the world.

I asked her if I could give her a ride home, and she said, "Of course not. I came with my friends, and I will leave with them." In spite of my brashness, I was able to get her phone number. The next day I called her, and we made a date that night to go to the New Haven drive-in theater, a place where we could have a conversation in English rather than my stilted French. We had five more dates that summer, and I thought I was hitting it pretty well.

On our last date that summer, she told me that she was actually in love with somebody else and she would not see me again as she was leaving for Paris in three days for a year of study abroad. This was a challenge. The next day I went down to the Vermont Bookstore and purchased a bon voyage card and sent it to her with the inscription: "Je t'aime encore et toujours" (I love you now and for always). I still use that phrase today. She went on her way, and I did not hear from her for several months. My memory of her was still strong but was fading away when I received a letter addressed to "Peter Langrocque, Lake Dunmore, Vermont." The good old Lake Dunmore post office, a summer office only, forwarded it from Lake Dunmore to Salisbury, Vermont, which forwarded it to New York at my parents' home, which forwarded it to my apartment in Chicago. This started a guarded relationship with weekly or bi-weekly letters. Over the course of the correspondence, we realized we had a lot in common and she agreed to come visit me when she returned to the states. Thus, the July 4th visit.

I am sure we had some good meals during that period, but culinary arts was not our major interest at that point. After the long weekend, she had to return to Washington where she was staying with her sister. As we waited for the bus on the first leg of her trip, I asked her what her favorite meat was. She responded, "Lamb." I said, "Me too." I think this was the ultimate question and answer that cemented our relationship. I then asked her how old she was. She told me, "Twenty-two." Being twenty-one and being aware of the statistics of women living longer than men, I blurted out, "Oh good. That means you'll be a widow for a shorter period of time." I guess that amounted to a form of proposal. Neither one of us took it further at that point, but two more visits in the summer before going back to school and a trip by her to Chicago at Thanksgiving time resulted in an engagement and our marriage on July 4th of the following year. Our meeting that night was sheer chance as we had no connection that would ever let us meet again. Had either she or I taken a different chair, our lives would have taken a different turn.

While the lamb question might have been a binder, an incident happened in Chicago which was just the reverse. Back at my apartment, Joann was taking a nap while I was preparing dinner. I had taken slices of eggplant, covered them with a tomato sauce and topped them with parmesan cheese and placed them in the oven until the cheese browned and the eggplant was done. It was my simple way of making eggplant parmigiano. I woke her and said we are having some dinner—I just made some eggplant parmigiano. Her response was, "I don't like eggplant." It was a blow to my culinary efforts, but I managed to survive it. Over the years, Joann has changed her mind about eggplant and it is a part of our regular eclectic diet.

By the time Thanksgiving came around, we had made a pact that she would come to Chicago and we would go to Botany Pond Bridge in the center quadrangle of the campus and I would ask her to marry me. If she said no, I would throw her in, and if I didn't ask her, she would throw me in. This was ultimately accomplished with neither one of us getting wet. It was a rather romantic time with snow falling gently on the campus, and I pulled a ring out of my vest pocket with a diamond that had originally been my grandfather's Masonic diamond, a gift to him for being an officer of the Grand Lodge of the State of New York.

The real surprise of the weekend, however, was my greeting Joann at Midway Airport as she got off her plane. Suddenly, an attractive young woman with purple-looking hair came off the ramp. I realized it was her. "Purple hair?" It turns out that she had a friend who had given her a rinse to accent her blond hair. The second rinse, however, had a chemical reaction, and it turned her hair purple. It wasn't the color of her hair that attracted me to her, and we got over that problem in short order.

CHAPTER 10

Vienna

Over the years, Joann and I traveled through much of Europe with Kim and Sue Sparks. Kim was a professor of languages at Middlebury College—his specialty being German, although he spoke Russian and several romance languages equally well. His favorite city was Vienna, where he had studied on a Fulbright before going on to teach at Princeton. While a student, he and his wife lived with Krista Esteahazy in an apartment she owned. During the year that they lived with her, they became very good friends and Krista became fond of both Susan and Kim, but especially Kim. This year of renting space in Krista's apartment built into a friendship that lasted throughout their lives.

Krista's apartment was inside the "ring" in the very center of Vienna. The "ring" was once the wall surrounding the city and has now been turned into its major beltway. Entry to the apartment was through oversized doors into a grand hallway. A small, caged elevator took you to the third floor and to Krista's apartment. Her apartment was like a museum with furniture and paintings going back to the days of the Austro-Hungarian Empire where her husband's father had been Minister of Finance. Krista was widowed. She was a small, tremendously energetic woman in her late 60s and a power in her own right (she represented Austria at the Beijing women's conference and as a poll watcher in Cambodia). While she loved the Sparks, she was not necessarily enamored of American tourists.

On our first visit to Vienna, Joann and I met up with the Sparks, who were staying with Krista while Kim was doing some research for his work on Vienna. He arranged for us to have cocktails at Krista's apartment and then have her join us for dinner at a local restaurant. When we arrived at her apartment, she was most gracious yet a bit hesitant in that she perceived us as being American tourists. The cocktails, as usual, were very dry martinis straight up and made with Beefeater gin supplied by Kim. While having cocktails, we mentioned our previous night in Vienna—Joann and I had gone to the Vienna Opera House to see Fidelio, Beethoven's only opera. When we started talking about the opera, you could almost see Krista's mind working: "Here are some typical American tourists who can afford to pay the exorbitant prices to see the always-sold-out Vienna opera." We continued with our story. Earlier the previous day, we had taken a guided tour of the opera house, learning the history of its survival and rebuilding after World War II. It had survived a direct bomb hit. The tour had showed us some of the back-stage operations, as well as the orchestra, boxes and the grand front stairway and the adjoining lounges. We had seen the set for that night's performance of Fidelio being put together and had decided to try and get tickets for it. We had been unsuccessful as all of our inquiries were met with "sold out."

In the early evening, I had suggested we walk from our hotel over to the opera house with the hope that we might find some person trying to sell tickets to that night's performance near the front of the opera house. We had sometimes been lucky trying to buy tickets that way at Lincoln Center for the Metropolitan Opera in New York. We still had no luck. It had been still quite a while before the start of the opera when I'd noticed a line waiting to go into the opera house. I'd asked a young lady at the end of the line about it, who fortunately spoke English. She'd said that this was the line for standing room. Joann and I had looked at each other, nodded, and got in line. Rather than paying the $200 plus dollars for an orchestra seat, we had been early enough so that our wait paid off and we got into the opera house for standing room at the cost of about $5. We'd watched the opera from the side of the fourth balcony. As we were behind the back row, we'd actually been able to partially sit down on the shelf behind us. The view was much better than we'd expected, and we'd excitedly watched Fidelio.

When we told the story of our standing room evening, I looked at Krista, and it was almost as if a light switch went on. You could see that she decided that if we were friends of the Sparks and were willing to undergo standing room at the opera to see Fidelio, we must be okay. There started our long friendship with Krista.

The next time I came to Vienna was to participate as an arbitrator in the Willem Vis Arbitration Moot. This competition is held each Easter week between law schools from around the globe. When I first started in 2000, there were about forty teams. This has grown to approximately 400 teams from seventy-five countries. The competition is held in English; the language universally used in international arbitration. Each school has four arguments—two for the claimant and two for the respondent. The arguments take place before a panel of three arbitrators who give individual point scores to the participants. The arbitrators consist of professors and lawyers from around the world. They pay their own way, and each night of the arbitration, some law firm or organization and sometimes an embassy throws a cocktail party that allows not only legal networking but also the meeting of friends from around the world.

After each team has completed its four arguments in the general rounds, the total points of the participating teams are totaled, and the top sixty-four teams go into a March madness-like single elimination tournament. Finals are argued before a panel of internationally known arbitrators at the exhibition hall at the Prater before a banquet crowd of 2,000 people.

My practice deals with arbitration on a relatively infrequent basis, and I am always an advocate and not an arbitrator. However, after participating for twenty-five years in the role of arbitrator, with some of the best arbitrators from around the world as colleagues, a lot of arbitration law has rubbed off on me. While the networking function of the VIS competition has only occasionally been applicable to my practice, I find that interacting with the students satisfies my need to be a teacher. This chance to break bread and share libations—although hardly ever martinis—has become an important part of my life. I have made friends there I never would have had an opportunity to meet but for the VIS competition. It is encouraging to see young people from around the world competing like hell all day over an international commercial problem and then partying together all night. It gives me some hope that this next generation will help advance the world towards a more rational and peaceful existence.

One of the people I met there was Heintz Luber and his wife Heidi. The Lubers have an apartment in the inner ring. He is one of the founders of the international law firm Freshfields, and his firm hosts a large cocktail party for the arbitrators during the course of the competition.

It was at one of those parties where I met Heintz. In the course of the conversation I mentioned that I was from Vermont. He told me that when he was a Fulbright student in New York, as an accomplished Austria skier, he had been invited to teach skiing at Killington during his winter school vacations. This developed into a fondness for Vermont and Vermonters.

Each year it was his policy to hold a small dinner gathering at his home in honor of the three guest arbitrators who were to judge the finals. He would also invite a few other participants of the moot to this dinner. On two occasions, we were fortunate enough to be invited.

The invitation was for 6:00 pm and everyone arrived between 6:00 and 6:05 pm. As we approached Heintz's apartment, Pierre Karrer, a well-known international arbitrator from Switzerland, approached from the opposite direction. I noticed he was wearing a new hat, a black fedora that was a twin to the one I had purchased that day at a shop that only sold hats. He recognized my hat, and it turned out that he had bought his hat the same day from the same shop.

I remember passing by the shop, smoking a cigar and looking in the window. The proprietor suggested I come in, but I pointed to the cigar in my hand. She said, "No problem," and presented me with an ashtray on entering the shop. With such a welcome, I felt I had a duty to make a purchase. I wear that hat to this day.

Coming in Heintz's front door, there were four steps up to a room just above street level where we were greeted with champagne and caviar canapes. After general conversation, the twelve of us were invited to retreat down the same stairs that we came in on and down another few stairs into a dining room just below street level. The walls of the dining room were brick going back to the 14th century.

Dinner was served by two tuxedoed, white-gloved waiters. In front of each guest was a printed menu listing the guest's name and outlining the menu. One evening we had tafelspitz, a traditional Viennese specialty of boiled beef. The food was memorable but even more so were the memories of the setting and the people present. Behind the dining room, the Lubers owned underground rights to several cellars under other neighbor's properties. I am very sure these walls held many stories from over the six centuries of their existence.

Another occasion of sharing libations with Heintz Luber was one evening when we were heading back to our hotel and walking along the streets when we met Heintz and another couple. He insisted we come back to his apartment. We were escorted into his home, where he promptly opened bottles of champagne. Then, to my surprise, he pulled from his bookshelf *Addison County Justice*—my first book—to show it off to the couple who was with him. I would not be telling the truth if I said I wasn't pleased.

The most memorable experience involving Heintz—other than the dinners at his home—started when I received an email. "I know it's impossible for you to do this, but if by some odd chance you are in New York on September 10th, some of my friends who I met when I was a Fulbright scholar fifty years ago are throwing a reception for me at the Knickerbocker Club. I would love to have you and Joann join us. I realize it is probably impossible for you to do so, but I did want to invite you. Heintz."

I immediately made reservations to go to New York. The Knickerbocker Club, as I was soon to find out, is the oldest and most exclusive club in New York. It is located on the east side of Central Park in its original stone structure from the 19th Century. While it is dwarfed by its more modern neighbors, it still has a most distinguished look. Once again, we arrived right on time at 6:00 pm and were escorted into a room where there was a full bar. The bar was ignored as everybody was drinking champagne from flutes being passed by a waiter. We joined the crowd.

After an hour of meeting people and good conversation, we were invited into the next room where there was a Grand Steinway Piano. An internationally known pianist was seated at the piano and presented a concert for the fifty guests. These guests included an array of accomplished individuals—as one might suspect from those who were Fulbright scholars of fifty years ago. Among them was Judith Kay, the then Chief Judge of the New York State Court of Appeals, the curator of the Metropolitan Museum of Art, and Seth Rozner, a good friend from ABA matters who had taught Heintz at New York University when he was a student. The piano concert consisted of a Beethoven concerto, Gershwin's "Rhapsody in Blue" and finally a composition by the pianist himself. The concert was over at 8:00 pm. We all said goodbye to each other and went our way to find dinner in one of New York's numerous restaurants. It was such a civilized way of celebrating a 50th scholarly anniversary.

On another occasion at the Vis, I acted as the chair of a three-person panel which heard a team from Beijing, China. One of the participants was Lin Po, who did the best job as an oralist I had seen in the many arbitrations I had participated in. Her argument was especially good as it was in the first round of the general arguments. The arguments usually improve as the teams progress through the competition. I kept in touch with several members of the team as they proceeded through the general round. They advanced to the playoffs but did not make it to the final round. Ling Po, however, received one of the individual rewards as an outstanding oralist.

In the course of talking with her after her first presentation—a practice where the arbitrators could make suggestions and help the students hone their next arguments—I learned that she would be in graduate school at Harvard the next year. I invited her to come up and visit us in Vermont. After the competition and returning to Vermont, I kept in touch with her while she was in Cambridge. Every time I would suggest that I had a friend coming up from Boston who could give her a ride to and from Vermont for a visit, she would decline, saying she had to study. She was a person who was not satisfied with being good or even excellent. She had to be perfect. Her goal was to be at the very top. At the end of the year, she found herself with a two-week hiatus between finishing at Harvard and moving on to Sweden where she had a one-year internship with a Swedish arbitration organization.

She was finally persuaded to come to Vermont, where she stayed with us for those two weeks. While she was staying with us, I had to argue a case in the Vermont Supreme Court. Over the years, I have argued more than 200 cases before the Court. Because of my familiarity with the Court, I was able, before starting my argument, to introduce Lin Po as a visiting attorney from Beijing. The Supreme Court welcomed her, and she stayed to listen to the argument.

Two days later, accompanied by Lin Po, I was arguing a motion in the trial court in Middlebury. After I finished my argument, Lin complimented me and said I made a very good argument, especially considering I was taking the minority position. She knew more about what I was arguing than I did.

She told me that she was planning after her year in Sweden to go back to Beijing to be with her husband and have the one child they were then permitted to have under Chinese law. Unfortunately, we have not kept in touch after her two weeks' visit.

I have had the good fortune to host other arbitrators from time to time at my home in Vermont. They came from diverse places, such as Stuttgart, Moscow, Dubai, Thailand, and Australia. I have also visited with participants from the Vis at their homes in Germany, the Netherlands, and Belgium.

With Joann and Kim and Sue Sparks, we planned to drive south from Vienna on a trip into Tuscany to enjoy the cuisine of the region. We rented a car and headed south towards Italy. On the way, we stopped and saw the "iceman." The "iceman" was found frozen in a glacier ravine still in his animal skin clothing and with his weapon. His death had actually dated back 50,000 years before the thawing glacier allowed its discovery. He was found on the borderline between Austria and Italy, and this resulted in both legal and diplomatic contests. Seeing its careful preservation gave us a picture of our own insignificance—given both the glacial history and the political history of this area.

Traveling further south, we visited the tourist town of San Gimignano. We were planning to stay there, but we somehow got on the wrong road, which led us to the main center of the town where no cars were allowed. We turned around and went out a one-way street the wrong way and somehow managed to get back on the main highway. We changed our minds about staying there and decided we would spend the night in Poggibonsi, a nearby commercial town. In Poggibonsi, we found a hotel. (An aside, Poggibonsi was also the location for the play "Love Goes to Press" by the World War II female correspondents, Virginia Coles and Martha Gelhorn—both amazing women.) Our Michelin guidebook showed only one restaurant with a single fork. We asked the front desk of the hotel to call and make a reservation for us. We arrived at the restaurant and were the first people there. We did not realize how lucky we were to get a table until we noticed that within the next half hour every single table was filled. While we were looking at the menus, a young man, maybe fifteen, came over and excitedly told us that they had just gotten portabella mushrooms from the mountains that day and by all means we should try them. We ordered them as an appetizer, and his excitement was justified. This was the start to one of the most memorable meals I have ever had. We ordered a Steak Florentine for four and were then shown a three-pound single cut of beef for our approval before grilling. It was then rubbed with lemon and salt and grilled on an open flame to perfection. It was sliced at the table and served equally to the four of us. It was, without a doubt, the singular best steak I have ever eaten. I have never been able to duplicate the experience.

After dinner, we went back to our hotel where I still had two pints of our Vermont farm maple syrup. Leaving our wives at the hotel, Kim and I went back to the restaurant and presented the chef, who had actually served the steak, a pint of the maple syrup as a small gift of appreciation. He had never seen maple syrup before, and we explained to him how it was made. He then offered us a dessert, but in lieu of that we settled on a grappa. The maple syrup was taken back to the kitchen, and we could see through the glass in the kitchen door that the entire cooking staff was standing with spoons sampling the maple syrup and tasting it for the first time.

I must tell one of my favorite stories about Kim Sparks and his need for house sitters when he headed off to Europe. Two young female students had volunteered to live in his house and take care of it for the six to eight weeks that he would be away. Kim had free-range chickens on his farm, and the young ladies were given instructions on how to feed them and to gather the eggs for their own use. One day they woke to the sound of a chicken clucking loudly as it tried to escape the clutches of a neighbor's dog. The dog caught it. Before they could rescue it, the chicken had been partially plucked and had suffered a couple of tooth puncture marks. The two young house sitters were not prepared for this type of (what appeared to them to be) major crisis. Rescuing the partially plucked, injured chicken, they decided the only thing they could do was to call the vet. The vet in town was a very competent Harley-Street type veterinarian: Donald Petty, who was capable of doing high quality work on small animals. His advice originally would have been to tell them to simply ring the chicken's neck and make a good chicken stew. He, however, detected the panic in their voices and said, "Bring it over and I'll see what I can do." The chicken arrived missing some feathers and a couple of minor puncture wounds, though otherwise it appeared to be in good health. He dabbled a little bit of iodine on the wounds, gave it back to the girls, and said that he thought the chicken would make it. As chickens run a very high body temperature, there was little chance of infection. The chicken did well, and they were very much relieved. There were no further chicken incidents.

When the Sparks arrived home, the two students decided they had to confess to them the problems they had with the dog and the chicken. After they related their panic-stricken story, Kim told them that they had done the right thing and not to have any worries about it. Thankfully, Don Petty had an appropriate sense of humor and did not send a bill to the Sparks.

On the Sunday after he got home, Kim went down to the local store to pick up *The New York Times.* As he greeted some local friends in the store, he noticed they were chuckling. He asked them what was so funny, and they said, "We understand you take your chickens to Dr. Petty." Kim could only laugh, and they all had a good joke about their exclusive veterinarian tending to the ills of Kim's chicken while he was away.

One of my good friends at the bar—both legal and otherwise—is Peter Martin. Peter had been a paratrooper in the U.S. Army before going to law school. He is strongly patriotic, and he believes everyone has a duty to work hard and support our government. He is conservative, not always logical, and hates able-bodied people who are on welfare rather than working. He often refers to these welfare recipients in politically incorrect terms. I refer to him as my "equal opportunity bigot."

Inside, he is one of the most kind and generous people I have ever met. On one occasion, he arranged for a luncheon for three lonely, aging World War II veterans who he was acquainted with. None of them knew each other, but his thoughtfulness and kindness allowed them to develop new friends—all sharing old memories.

Peter likes his martinis if you can call a vodka martini with a slice of lime a martini. We often share martinis (I stick with gin) before lunch along with oysters on the half shell at Jeff's Restaurant in Saint Albans. Saint Albans is Peter's home and the site of his practice. Invariably, we would have lunch together when I had a case that took me there.

Two female lawyers—one from Stuttgart, Germany, and one from Moscow, Russia—were visiting my home. I had met them and worked with them at the Vis Moot in Vienna. During their visit, I took the day off to give them a tour through much of northern Vermont. I had arranged it so we would be in St. Albans at noon where we were to meet Peter for lunch at Jeff's. After ordering a vodka martini for himself and a real martini for me and lesser strength libations for our two guests, Peter said to our visiting colleagues, "I have a present for you." He proceeded to pull from his pants pocket two glass maple leaves filled with maple syrup. As he presented one of his gifts, I noticed that my colleague from Stuttgart, Anna Marie Gosshaus, had a sparkle in her eye, and she teased Peter by saying, "What else have you got in your pocket?" Peter didn't say a word, but he reached into his belt and pulled out a 38-caliber revolver and laid it on the table. If you can imagine two fully surprised and bug-eyed lawyers from Russia and Germany, you would still be underrating the reaction they had.

Peter always carried heat with him. I have tried to explain to him that the best way to get shot is to carry a handgun with you. He's never listened to my advice. Part of Peter's conservative beliefs include a strong faith in the Second Amendment. Vermont is probably the one liberal state in the union that has no restrictions on owning or carrying firearms. Until fairly recently, there was no security at the courthouses, and Peter was upset when security measures were initiated at the courthouses and he was no longer allowed to enter armed with a concealed weapon. He was not alone in his frustration at the advancement of security. Another St. Albans lawyer, Howard Van

Benthuysen, had to give up carrying a concealed weapon when coming into the courthouse, even when he became a judge.

When I first started practice, for some reason, which I cannot explain why today, many, if not most, lawyers kept a loaded handgun in their desk drawer. I know of no time when one was ever used, but for some reason it was a piece of equipment that many lawyers felt was appropriate. I kept a loaded 38-caliber revolver in my desk. One day I realized that my secretary, who is a wonderful person, occasionally had suicidal thoughts. I said to myself, "What in hell am I doing with a loaded revolver in my desk drawer?" I sold that revolver, and I have never owned another handgun since.

Peter is one person who truly appreciates the importance of breaking bread and sharing libations in maintaining a long-standing and close friendship.

To me, the height of luxury is a late-night supper after the opera. When in Vienna, we have a favorite—a little Italian restaurant called Don Carlos, just a short way up the Galleria across the road from the Opera House. As I have been a patron for many years, albeit only during Easter week when I am there for the VIS competition, they remember me, and the greeting is always most cordial. If there is a delay in the seating, our party is presented with a complimentary glass of prosecco.

This particular evening, after seeing The Elixir of Love, Joann and I, together with old friends King and Esther Burnett who were also in Vienna for the Vis moot, had just settled in for our late dinner at Don Carlos. The restaurant has two rooms. The main dining room has eight tables and can hold no more than twenty-odd people. There is another room of similar size that can hold another twenty people. This night everything was centered in the main dining room, including a birthday party for a girl celebrating her sixteenth birthday. At one point, the head waiter with a beautiful tenor voice sang to the birthday girl a Neapolitan love song. As he was finishing, in came the baritone Ambrogio Maestro who had just sung the role of Dulcamara, a role which can be characterized as a snake oil salesman who convinces poor Nemaorino that a bottle of cheap Bordeaux is really a magical elixir. As he moved to his table, he nodded at the waiter, acknowledging his joyful singing. The waiter, having finished singing to the birthday girl, turned and sang another less romantic song to Maestro. At this point, Maestro stood up and, in response to the waiter, sang an aria from The Elixir of Love. His voice filled the room to a level I could never have imagined. The place was physically vibrating with the power of his voice. He finished the song, and we all returned to our dinner while Maestro decided he would go outside and have a cigarette. The seeming incompatibility of a cigarette and a world-class operatic voice is apparently not so incompatible after all.

CHAPTER 11

Jamaica

The Shoreham Cooperative apple facility on Route 22A was the biggest apple cooperative east of the Mississippi. Each year, a half-million boxes of apples were stored and processed as fresh fruit. Champlain Valley is known for the best Macintosh apples in the world. Growing and marketing them is a year-round activity. All of this work is dependent upon a successful harvest season. The harvest requires experienced pickers who have the skills and agility to treat the fruit gently when they are lifted off the trees. I say lifted off because that is the motion that is required to have the fruit retain their stems and reduce the pressure that the fingers exert in a pulling move that can damage the fruit. It may sound counterintuitive, but putting a bruised apple into a picking bag eventually involves more cost by way of handling and storage than its salvage value for cider. Economically, it is better that a damaged apple be thrown to the ground than placed into the picking bucket.

Before the 1930s and well into the 40s and 50s, Vermont's rural economy was such that the picking was handled by local people who looked forward to earning some extra money. Picking is a peak-loading operation, and a Macintosh apple has a window of little more than twenty-one days to be picked at its prime. Other varieties expand that window a little bit.

After the end of World War II, the local labor supply of pickers declined in numbers. The growers with expanded orchards were in need of, and were able to, tap a new harvest labor force. This was from the British West Indies through a guest visitor plan. The H-2 program, as it was called, had been initiated during World War II to import labor to help in war production, but it expanded to agriculture in the 1950s This harvest labor program ran smoothly until the mid-70s when the Department of Labor decided to try and fill these short-term seasonal jobs with unemployed Americans.

Simply, there was no way to marshal a sufficient U.S. workforce from the unemployed to deal with the labor-intensive four-to-six-week period required for picking apples. Potential U.S. workers were not used to physical outdoor work, and with the season being so short, they were reluctant to temporarily relocate and live at the orchards. The apples would come off the tree—the trick was to get them into the boxes, and this required a skilled and dependable workforce. Unfortunately, the Department of Labor did not agree, and for the next sixteen years, I was involved in litigation, with the Department of Labor. (The interesting and somewhat fascinating story of the litigation is set out in my book *Beyond the Courthouse*.) As a result of the course of this litigation each year I would journey to the Caribbean where I would attend the annual negotiations between the West India Labor Organization and the employers. This is just background for the delightful and often fascinating negotiations where I was representing the Shoreham Coop. The members of the Shoreham Coop utilized about 300 workers of the 9,000 to 12,000 who came to the eastern United States under the H-2 program to pick apples. Many of the workers, at the end of apple picking, transferred to cut sugar cane in Florida. These were racially difficult times, and I am glad to say the Shoreham Coop's owners were much more sensitive to the different needs of the workers. Some of the other growers and particularly one of the four major sugar growers in Florida were much less sensitive. As far as sugar cane cutting, the relationship ended after a story featuring the latter sugar cane company's operation and its treatment of workers appeared on one of the national network news shows. After the feedback from that television presentation, all the growers switched to mechanical harvesting, destroying much needed work for the Jamaicans. However, Vermont farmers use British West Indies workers to harvest their crops to this day.

Of the sixteen years I participated in negotiations dealing with the underlying employment contract, fourteen of the meetings were held in Jamaica, one in Barbados, and one in Saint Lucia. The meetings in Jamaica were usually held at the Shaw Park Hotel in Ocho Rios. I would fly from Boston into the tourist mecca of Montego Bay and then on debarkation be greeted with a rum punch. There is nothing like a good rum punch to lighten the atmosphere and raise the moods of all involved. I would then catch a ride with some of the employers on the three-hour drive along the north coast to Ocho Rios.

On route, we would stop at a roadside stand for jerk chicken. I have had jerk chicken in many places, but nothing in my memory ever equals the taste of that chicken cooked outside on an open fire and eaten without ceremony while sitting on benches surrounding a small shack, drinking a cold Red Stripe beer and enjoying good company.

The Shaw Park Hotel had once been the beach house for the main hotel that was further inland from the beach. The hotel was abandoned due to the increasing success of the beach house and its seaside restaurant and bar. The rooms were within a hundred feet from the edge of the water, with doors that opened right onto the beach. My memories of these week-long negotiations are filled with formal meetings but with the real work being done informally over drinks or meals with people from both sides of the negotiations. Many of them on both sides became my good friends.

Notably was Harold Edwards, the chief liaison officer for the British West Indies Labor Organization. Most mornings we would meet for a swim at 7:00 am and casually swim out into the bay where the fresh and cool waters coming off the mountain in the White River mix with the warm salt waters of the bay. It was like swimming through a marble cake. Harold and I, while swimming, would discuss the issues of the day and plot out our approaches for the formal meetings. We would then dress and meet for breakfast. It was there where he introduced me to some Caribbean fruits that I had never been familiar with but now enjoy as a special treat whenever I get them. My favorite being the large, flavorful papaya picked from the tree ripe with its unparalleled flavor.

After a day of negotiations, I would dress for dinner and head down to the bar on the edge of the beach next to the dining room. Here, in the evening, there was music, dancing and various entertainments. It was at this bar where I learned to drink Wray and Nephew Overproof White Rum over ice with a squeeze of lime. Today I drink it when I can get it, and each time I take that first sip, I feel like I am being transported back to the Shaw Park Hotel.

Harold was a good friend of the Governor General, Sir Florizel Glasspole. Sometime during the negotiations, he would invite me to join him and go across to the south side of the island to Kingston to meet with the governor general at King's House. On the way across the island, we would go through Fern Gully and up across the top of the mountains that separated Ocho Rios and Kingston. Near the top of the pass, we would stop on the roadside where somebody had a small fire and was roasting salted cod and yams. The memory of the flavor of a piece of roasted salted cod partially charred along with the yam and a can of Red Stripe beer is always reminiscent of my friendship with Harold Edwards.

Harold also introduced me to another libation that still holds a favorite place in my heart and my taste buds. It had been a long day of sensitive negotiations, with Harold leading the charge for better conditions for the workers and the employers trying to deal with those demands in a financially economical way. After dinner, Harold invited me to his room to continue our discussion. When I arrived, he brought out a bottle of Cardinal Mendoza, a Spanish brandy. I soon learned to appreciate the rich taste of a quality Spanish brandy, different from the clearness of a French cognac (a bit fuller and of many tastes). Cardinal Mendoza is not usually carried by the Vermont state liquor stores, so I can only obtain it from specialty liquor stores when I am in big cities. Sometimes I can get a bottle of Duke of Albuquerque, another brandy of the same quality. Whenever I find this, I buy an extra bottle. The extra bottle was a gift for Harold when I met him in Washington, D.C., in the embassy-like offices of the Central Labor Organization.

At the end of the week of negotiations, a luncheon was put on by the Central Labor Organization. Besides the participants in the negotiations, there were invited guests from Kingston, including the minister who carried the Portfolio of Sports and Labor, and sometimes the prime minister, himself. I say him because for all the years I was there the prime minister was a male. However, the minister who held the Portfolio of Sports and Labor was Portia Simpson, a beautiful, brilliant Black woman. She later became the first female prime minister of Jamaica. While she held the labor portfolio, I had the pleasure of entertaining her at my farm when the annual delegation from Jamaica visited the operations of the apple orchards of the Northeast.

On another visitation of the delegation and before a scheduled dinner at the Waybury Inn, I invited them to my house for drinks. On route we passed the Addison County Commission Sales, which has a twice-weekly auction of cull cows and bob calves. It was apparent that a sale was going on, and I suggested that they might want to see a cattle auction in action. We entered the pit area where the cattle are sold. This consists of a small chute through which cattle pass into the sale ring. The weight of the animals is announced, and the bidding moves very rapidly at so much a pound. The animals are sold to various buyers from different meat packing houses and exited from the sale ring into various pens. The ring is surrounded by a small stand for the buyers and a smattering of farmers, some of whom may have consigned the cattle going through the ring. I enjoyed the look of astonishment as I arrived with four Black men dressed in suits to observe the auction in rural Vermont.

As I said, through the sixteen years of negotiations, I developed many friendships—some of which continue to this day. One of these persons was Earl Whyte, the regional liaison officer who worked directly with the workers when they were here in Vermont. Whenever he visited, he would bring me a bottle of the Wray and Nephew Overproof White Rum. He knew I enjoyed it and knew that it was unavailable in Vermont. Earl also introduced me to some Jamaicans who were not directly tied to the Central Labor Organization. Among these were Pat Salter and his wife, Ivy. Pat was in charge of the water system that supplied Kingston. He had a home in one of the nicer sections of Kingston. Kingston, as a capital of a third-world country, has a broad mixture of housing, from the grounds of Kings House to the tar paper squatter shacks on the outskirts of Kingston.

Pat was also involved in a youth orchestra. On one trip, when I was invited to a party at Pat and Ivy's home, I brought down my son's abandoned clarinet and my old saxophone and donated them to the Youth Orchestra as a host gift. I had first met Pat and Ivy when they visited us in company with

Earl and his wife, Carol, at the farm.

I had first met Carol when she came to the farm with Earl. I had the opportunity to cook some Jamaican Escovitch from a recipe, which I had learned from talking to a chef at the Shaw Park Hotel. (Escovitch, as well as goat curry, are two of my favorite Jamaican specialties.)

The making of Escovitch is really simple. Usually, it is made of small panfish. I do not know the names of the fish that are used in Jamaica, but I make it in Vermont with filets of sunfish or crappies—often caught through the ice in the winter. The fish are floured, salt and peppered, and then fried in a pan in a small amount of cooking oil. I use a large cast iron skillet that I get very hot so the fish will be crispy and cooked in a very short period of time. Once they are done, they are removed and set aside. In the same cast iron skillet, I add thin strips of sweet peppers and white onions and sauté them until they are soft, scraping the residue from the frying into the mixture. I then add some white vinegar and Jamaican hot sauce. I let this mixture cook for a few minutes and then pour it over the fish that I had arranged on a platter. The dish can be served hot or cold. They never taste exactly the same but are always good.

When I made it for Earl and Carol, I did not have any pan fish, but I had a large number of small trout that I had caught from the stream running through the farm. I followed the same procedure, but instead of the sunfish and crappies, there were the small brook trout. It turned out well. I will always remember Carol saying, "If somebody told me yesterday that I would be eating Escovitch this good in Vermont and made by a honky, I would not have believed it."

In January of 2020, the H-2 program held its celebration in Jamaica in honor of its 75th anniversary. This program, which allowed Jamaicans to come to work in the U.S. for the harvest season, was an important financial source of hard currency for Jamaica. The Jamaican workers were usually rural Jamaicans who had small subsistence farms throughout the island. They looked forward to their trip to the United States each year as this gave them an opportunity to earn an amount of hard cash in a relatively short period of time. It would have taken them almost a year to earn the same amount in rural Jamaica. With the money they earned, they would buy things to take home—things that they could not normally have afforded or obtained in Jamaica. Money that they earned often went into improving their homes and farms. Personally, I know of no better way to improve international relations than to have the people of one country receive financial benefits from another country while that host second country benefits from their labor and short-term visit. It certainly worked here.

In many cases, the workers would come back to pick apples for thirty years, becoming true friends of the growers they worked for. One friendship I recall was the basis for two stories about a grower named Bo Patterson. One of the workers damaged his pants on the upward-bound trip to Vermont. When he arrived, Bo's wife indicated that she would repair the pants for him and did so. The next day, when he went to the house to retrieve them, he found her ironing his repaired slacks before she would turn them over. The second instance was when Bo's wife passed, and he paid to fly this worker to Vermont to read a psalm at her funeral.

Because of my activities in the negotiations over the years and the role I played in designing the legal framework that saved the program, I was invited as a guest of honor at the 75th anniversary celebration. I accepted the invitation and went to a resort on the north side of the island. I was supposed to meet with the prime minister, but logistics did not work out and I did not get that opportunity. However, I did get to see many old friends—

both inside and outside of the government. I also received an invitation to visit Pat and Ivy Salters' beach house on the southeast side of the island. Earl and Carol Whyte picked me up and we drove out to the Salter's vacation home. Ivy, remembering my fondness for goat curry, prepared for me the best goat curry I've ever had.

As I look back over my experience with Jamaica and the many wonderful experiences I had, there are a few that especially stick out. I remember the shared meals, the shared drinks, working with people whom I got to know, and how important the breaking of bread and the enjoyment of shared libations were in cementing those friendships.

One morning, after negotiations with the British West Indies Labor Board Bo Patterson from the Shoreham Coop, Marvin Peck, the head of the New England Apple Council, and I decided to take a ride through the countryside. While touring back roads, we stopped at what was called a supermarket—a supermarket in Jamaica is usually nothing more than a corrugated metal shack with a refrigerator full of cold beer. Some also sell white rum. On that day I was in a white rum mood, and we investigated more than one supermarket. The roads we traveled were only one car wide, and we slowed almost to a stop when carefully passing the car coming in the other direction. The universal practice is as you approach a curve, hit the horn—beep, beep—and carry on. Happily, I followed this practice, and we continued beep beeping down the roadway known as Devil's Racecourse.

At one supermarket, we were approached by a local. "Come on into the back room." This was a bigger operation, having two rooms and a kitchen. After another white rum, I found myself in the kitchen helping the chef make Jamaican meat patties. They are a spicy, meat-filled crescent of pastry, and they go with any beverage. After finishing up the patties and while under the influence of another white rum, I agreed to arm wrestle the chef. Even without the white rum I would have lost.

There is one more story I have to share. My next-to-last meeting was the year that Harold Edwards retired. He had been awarded an O.B.E., on the Queen's list. While Jamaica is an independent nation, it is still a part of the British Commonwealth. However, this did not turn out to be his swan song as he did not completely leave the organization. He was hired back as a consultant. The following year at the annual banquet, Harold was back at the head table.

Harold was a devout Roman Catholic. He knew I was not a religious person, but at the cocktail party preceding the annual banquet, he asked me if I would be willing to say the benediction. I told him that I really was not the person that should be doing that and suggested that he ask one of the other growers. I continued to enjoy the libations of the cocktail party and was in a fine metal when we sat down at the tables. Harold was at the end of the slightly raised front table where the chair and other members of the labor board, as well as invited guests from the government, sat. As the guests had all seated themselves, Tony Irons, who was the chair of the labor board, rose and announced over the loudspeaker, "Mr. Peter Langrock will deliver the benediction." I had prepared nothing, I was taken by surprise, but I could hardly decline. As I walked past Harold at the end of the podium, he smiled and said to me sotto voce, "A parting shot." I managed to say appropriate words without involving too much theology and everybody was satisfied. I will never forget, however, Harold simply saying: "a parting shot."

CHAPTER 12

Law and Town Stories

In 1973, the Uniform Law Commission met in Vail, Colorado. The week-long conference is held in different places each year, and oftentimes we turn it into a family vacation. This was my first trip to Colorado, and I planned to take advantage of it by bringing along a fly rod in anticipation of its legendary trout streams.

The work starts on Saturday, but on Friday night there is a cocktail reception—an opportunity that allows for the renewal of old friendships and meeting of new commissioners. I was torn by two choices. One was to go to the reception and the other was to try out my fly rod on the stream that flows directly through Vail village. I decided to do both.

We had rented a unit in a small condo that looked over the convention area where the reception was held. I dressed appropriately and went down to enjoy the reception. After several drinks, I decided to go back to the condo, put on my fishing gear, including waders, grab my fly rod, and give the stream a quick try before dark.

The condo and reception area were both within viewing distance of the stream. In stepping into the water, I was in full view of both. I tied on a small streamer and waded into the center of the stream. Due to the effects of the libations at the reception, I tried to be extra careful as I walked down the calf-leg depth of water flowing over the rocky streambed while looking for a likely spot for a trout to hide.

I held the rod back over my shoulder, and unknown to me my line dangled into the water trailing the streamer fly. I had not gone more than ten yards when suddenly my rod jerked. Accidently, I had tempted a 14" rainbow trout to attack the fly and turning around managed to land it. I could not resist the temptation. I picked up the trout, and in waders marched along the base of the outdoor reception, which was still in full swing. It was great fun to walk by dressed in fishing gear and not my suit of a few minutes before with my rod and a nice rainbow trout in hand accompanied by a big smile on my face. The fish later ended up in a frying pan in our condo.

The next day, Joann and I, with our four-year-old son, Eric, were walking along one of Vail's sidewalks. The sides of the walkway were built with a railroad tie construction holding back the bank with grass leading from the ties to the edge of the buildings. The height of the railroad ties was just a foot below my son's sight line. Suddenly he stopped and looked at a mole emerging from the grass and running along the top of the ties. He exclaimed with excitement, "Look, Mommy, an elephant!" He had a stuffed three-inch elephant toy and had seen pictures of elephants with their long trunks but had never seen one alive. The long nose of the mole and its gray fur convinced him that he was seeing a live elephant for the first time. It taught me a lesson: "The matter of perspective is always in the eye of the beholder."

Sharing drinks and meals among friends is always a large part of the fun side of the meeting. Commissioners work seriously and put in six full days of examining and drafting proposed uniform legislation. During the day, the commissioners usually meet as a committee of the whole, with 150 to 200 commissioners actively engaged in serious debate. It was an accepted practice to occasionally take a break from this regimen and have private visits with fellow commissioners.

One of my dear friends was from Virginia, Brockenridge Lamb. Brocky, as he was called, was a marvelous character. He had attended the University of Virginia, where he had a dorm room on the edge of the green in the center of the campus. He loved to tell the story about the time he drove a motorcycle across the green up to his room and survived the disciplinary repercussions from doing so.

During one afternoon meeting, Brocky passed by my seat and handed me a note. I opened the note and it said, "Peter, I have a Virginia gentleman up in my room who would like to meet with you." Not being quite sure what this was all about, I left the meeting and went to his room. As I knocked on the door, his lovely wife opened it and welcomed me. She was used to Brocky and his antics and both loved and tolerated him. It turns out that the Virginia gentleman he was talking about was a bottle of Virginia Gentleman bourbon whiskey, and he promptly poured me a generous portion. That started a tradition. At every subsequent conference, on some afternoon I would get an invitation from Brocky to join him and his friend, the Virginia Gentleman. The libations we shared cemented a friendship that lasted through the rest of his life.

Brocky had a great sense of timing and a great sense of humor. He did not often speak from the floor of the conference, but when he did his comments were always apropos and usually humorous. My favorite occurred when the conference was taking up the Uniform Trust Code. The members of the Drafting Committee were sitting on the podium. They took turns reading each section of the proposed act line-by-line, word-for-word before opening the section up for discussion. On this particular occasion, the paragraph under consideration involved the ability to set up a testimony trust to care for one's surviving pets. The proposal limited the duration of the trust to thirty years.

John Langbine first served as a commissioner from Illinois when he was a professor at the University of Chicago Law School and then as a commissioner from Connecticut when he moved to Yale University. John was a true scholar and one with mental acuity a quantum leap over even the very bright group of commissioners. John was assigned the reading of the paragraph dealing with the trust for animals. He started to read it hesitantly but could not keep a straight face and started to giggle halfway through it. This brought a wave of laughter among the commissioners. John stopped and started to read it again. This time he had not gotten into it as far as he had the first time before he started actually giggling like a teenager. At this point, the conference joined him in riotous laughter themselves. Undaunted, John went to try and read it a third time. He hardly had gotten six words out of his mouth when the giggles returned, and by this time people were laughing so hard that some actually started to fall from their chairs.

The chair had to assign somebody else to successfully finish reading the section. As debate on the section was called for, Brocky was recognized from the chair. "I don't know about that thirty-year limitation. I come from the Chesapeake Bay area, and we've got turtles down there that live seven hundred years." This brought the house to another roar of laughter.

At the Annual Meeting of the Uniform Law Conference, there is a gala party to raise funds for its Foundation. The foundation is a registered charitable organization and thus cannot provide direct support for any lobbying. It does, however, provide funds for some of the research work that goes into the background for creating the proposed uniform laws. At several of these galas, there has been an auction of items donated by commissioners, and I often served as the auctioneer. I have a pretty good patter, but without being trained in voice, I can go on for only a limited time before my voice gives out.

When I was conducting the auction, Joann was in the audience with a smile on her face, knowing that I cannot either advise her on bidding or object to any bids she might make. On three occasions I have had to knock down an item to her at a rather extended price. One of these items resulted in twenty lobsters donated by Louis Vivades of Maine to be shipped to us in Vermont by Federal Express. Louis was a noted trial lawyer who successfully represented a Maine hunter who had accidentally shot and killed a woman hanging out her laundry when she waved a white towel and the hunter thought it was the tail flag of a deer. I do not know the details of the defense, but it was a case that attracted national attention. The resulting twenty lobsters called for us to host a lobster bake for eighteen of our good friends. The bid was a small part of the cost of that evening.

On another occasion, Richard Long, who represented The Otesaga Resort Hotel in Cooperstown, New York, obtained a two-night donated stay at the hotel during the summer season for the auction. Joann's successful bid resulted in our taking a trip to Cooperstown, where we attended two operas at Glimmerglass. Glimmerglass' summer season was a favorite venue for the unlikely pairing of Supreme Court Justices Ruth Bader Ginsburg and Antonin Scalia.

Cooperstown is a marvelous experience in itself with the Fenimore Cooper Museum, Glimmerglass, and the Baseball Hall of Fame, all together in a beautiful upstate N.Y. rural area. The Otesaga Resort Hotel is a grand old hotel run on the American Plan where all meals at the hotel are included in the tariff. This was the same plan as the Lake Dunmore Hotel in Vermont where I spent all my summers growing up, working there until I was partway through law school. A feeling of nostalgia gripped me as I ordered my favorite, a spanish omelet for breakfast.

Of course we visited the Baseball Hall of Fame. The thing I remember most about the Hall of Fame is that they have one of the old wooden seats from Ebbets Field, the Brooklyn Dodgers home field on Bedford Avenue. It brought back memories of my mother, an ardent Dodgers fan, taking me to the games and seeing #42 Jackie Robinson making history.

On a third occasion, Gay Bamberger, the publicist for the Uniform Law Conference, donated her apartment on East 73rd Street in Manhattan for the Thanksgiving weekend when she left New York City for a family weekend. It turned out to be a fun weekend where we would shop for exotic food at small gourmet groceries in the neighborhood, making us feel like New Yorkers for a few days. On Thanksgiving Eve, we watched Macy's parade balloons being filled and held down by cables on the side streets off the west side of Central Park. The next day we watched the parade with hundreds of thousands of others.

The highlight of the weekend was a dinner at the apartment of one of King Burnett's daughters. King served a two-year term as the president of the Uniform Law conference. He had asked me to serve as his vice-president, and after spending time together, we became even better friends. It turned out he was going to be in New York the same Thanksgiving weekend. King has three daughters Erin, Laurie, and Mara. It was Mara's apartment where Thanksgiving dinner was planned. Erin, who was joining us, was a journalist who worked her way up through the field of television reporters from Bloomberg to CNBC and was finally the anchor on CNN's Erin Burnett Out Front—CNN's leading early evening news program.

As King is a bit of a wine connoisseur, we did not participate in martinis that night but went through several bottles of different wines. The

Thanksgiving dinner was not going to be a turkey but rather two roasted ducks. When it came time for dinner, we were all in a jolly mood and the two ducks were presented to King on a platter, breast down as they had been cooked that way to ensure juicy breasts. King was in control of the carving knife and started to work on the ducks. As he started carving, he complained that there did not appear to be enough meat on the two ducks to feed the six of us. It was then we all realized that he was trying to carve the back of the ducks rather than the breasts. It was good wine. Turning them over remedied the problem and we had a wonderful dinner.

During the course of the evening, a parakeet that had the liberty to fly around the apartment decided to land squarely on top of King's bald head. The picture of that in my mind still makes me smile.

Each of Joann's bids led to the breaking of bread and sharing of libations with a group of friends, and I cherish her bids that brought it all about.

In 2020, the Uniform Law Conference met in Stowe, Vermont. As part of the host team, I was able to make a gift to each of the delegates of a half pint of maple syrup made on our farm. We have had a sugaring operation of one sort or another since we bought it in 1968. I have never been in charge of sugaring myself as it has either been done by neighbors making use of our sugarhouse or someone working for me on the farm operating the sugar operation on their own. Even today at ULC meetings people often fondly remember our gift of maple syrup.

Sugaring is a labor-intensive operation. It requires not only tapping the trees and tending to the boiling in the evaporator in the sugarhouse but includes maintaining the sugarhouse and gathering in excess of ten full cords of wood to burn under the evaporator. One of our neighbors for a while was Bud Bearor, and he made a family affair out of the operation as he had thirteen children and labor was not a problem. Now we have a more sophisticated system, including reverse osmosis, and our production has almost reached our 1,000-gallon goal. My only profit from the operation is whatever syrup I need for myself, my family, and friends. The 300 half pints I needed for the conference was stretching it a bit. We often bring a quart of syrup as a hostess gift when we go to someone's home rather than the traditional bottle of wine, and we often pack maple syrup in our luggage when we go to Europe as a gift to various people, many of whom have never tasted or even heard of maple syrup.

The American Law Institute was founded in 1923 to try and codify the American common law by way of a scholarly restatement of what the law is and, in some cases, what the law should be. It is a private organization and has self-selected about 3,500 members. For the most part, it is a collection of quality lawyers from around the country who are interested in law reform. As it is self-selecting, it sometimes can be a bit stuffy and is weighted heavily with federal judges, professors, and big-city lawyers from large firms. Many of the ULC commissioners have been elected to the organization, and they bring their strength from the floor of the conference to the floor of the ALI. Each year it meets for three days in May to discuss and approve the publishing of the various restatements of the law. It has also played a role in helping to create some statutory law, such as the Uniform Commercial Code. Usually, the meetings are held in Washington, D.C.—for many years at the Mayflower Hotel and more recently at the Ritz Carlton. However, at times, it meets on the west coast in San Francisco, and on rare occasions in Philadelphia that houses its headquarters.

At the annual meeting, there used to be a black-tie cocktail reception with a full bar and heavy hors d'oeuvres. The reception continues, but the black ties have almost disappeared. This is usually held at some significant venue such as a museum. The year it was held in Philadelphia, it was at a museum, housing a wonderful collection of impressionist works. Joann was with me, and after the reception, which was scheduled to end at 7:00 pm, we decided to have dinner at an Italian restaurant that had been recommended to us. Upon leaving the reception, on the front steps leading out of the museum, I ran into Kinvin Wroth, a professor from the University of Maine. I knew Kinvin through his work on the Vermont rules of criminal and civil procedure. I asked him if he would like to join us for dinner, and he said he would love to. I called the restaurant only to find out that they were completely booked. Upon telling this to Kinvin, rather than being disappointed, he said, "Do you know, the Phillies are in town." Both Joann and I are baseball fans and that was all that was needed for the three of us to grab a cab and go to the ballpark.

Just outside the gates at the ballpark, we ran into a person who was trying to sell three tickets to the game. The seats were on the first row of the upper deck on the third base side. The fact that Kinvin and I were both wearing tuxedos did not deter us at all from getting into the ballpark. We settled down in our seats and enjoyed hot dogs smeared with mustard and a cold beer. This was fine until the sixth inning when the skies opened up and we were sitting in the open top and got drenched with heavy rain. Everybody scattered, and we were unable to find a cab to take us back to the hotel. We were quite a sight getting into the subway in our totally soaked and mustard-stained tuxedos. We survived the soaking, and I will cherish the good memories surrounding hot dogs, mustard, rain, tuxedos, the Phillies, and Kinvin.

Charlie Welling, a commissioner from North Carolina, and I

often lunched together during the annual meeting of the Uniform Law Commission. Charlie once suggested that we lunch at a Cajun restaurant that he had heard about that had a talented chef, Paul Prudhomme—K. Paul's Kitchen. We found that it did not take reservations, but we took our chances and, after a short wait in line, we got a table. Our first look at the menu shouted out with their featured Cajun martinis. Of course we ordered them.

The martinis came to us served in a pint bell-jar loaded with ice and clear white liquor. The first taste told us all. One of the joys of drinking a martini is the first sip with its clean, clear taste that lingers for a moment after the liquid is swallowed. The surprising thing about the Cajun martini was this first clean, clear taste lingered and lingered and lingered. The sharpness of a jalapeño pepper added to the lingering flavor. It had been prepared by the soaking of jalapeño peppers in gin prior to its participation in the martini. It was magnificent. We decided to try the restaurant again, and the second and third times we tried the Cajun martini the reaction was the same.

As we were finishing our luncheon, I noticed the chef coming out and sitting at a table near the door to the kitchen. I went by his table, and in response to my complimentary remark he invited me to sit down and talk with him. I spent the next fifteen minutes in a wonderful conversation about cooking and Cajun food in particular. An unforgettable experience. This all occurred before Paul Prudhomme became a household name in gastronomic circles and became the international celebrity that he now is.

Some years later, I was back in New Orleans with Joann and K-Paul's Kitchen still took no reservations. After standing in line for thirty minutes, we were seated. The only way to get a table was to take your turn waiting in line. I remember this occasion especially as Joann ordered a haunch of rabbit with a mustard sauce. The flavors were unbelievable as she shared a taste of it with me. It was not only the best rabbit I had ever tasted, but it was one of the really great dishes I ever tried.

At a weekend meeting in New Orleans of a ULC Drafting Committee Meeting, we finished our work on Saturday and the scheduled meeting for Sunday morning was canceled. I found myself with a free morning before having to catch an early afternoon flight back to Vermont. I had heard of the famous "Breakfast at Brennan's" and decided to splurge.

I started with a Sazerac cocktail and then ordered "quail in a nest." This consisted of a roasted quail nestled in a hollow of fried shoestring potatoes. It was presented like a bird's nest with the quail in the middle. I had a half bottle of a Chardonnay to accompany it and then finished off my meal with Brennan's signature dessert: "bananas foster." Bananas foster was an invention of Brennan's and was named after one of its patrons, Richard Foster. I watched the bananas foster being made at the table, and I have often duplicated it at home. I melt some butter in a saucepan, add sliced bananas, and instead of brown sugar I add maple syrup. As a finishing touch it is flamed with rum or brandy and then poured over vanilla ice cream. It is simple to make and absolutely delicious.

My bill for breakfast was well outside of the ordinary range I spend for breakfast, but I rationalized it on the grounds that I had worked hard all weekend. My partners teased me about the amount I had charged to the firm's credit card for the breakfast, knowing full well that a large part of it was to be reimbursed.

CHAPTER 13

Deer and Other Meats

It was a Friday in November 1963, the day before the opening of deer season. I was at home getting ready to go off to dear camp with a fellow attorney, Gerry Trudeau. In the early 1960s, most service businesses closed during deer season. Going to a remote camp for a period of comradeship, libations, and a little hunting was an enshrined practice.

I was the state's attorney, and I received a call from a game warden. He had just apprehended two hunters from Montreal who had shot two doe for "camp meat," a common but illegal practice. The warden said they were ready to plead guilty to a charge of illegally taking a deer but would like to do so right away so they could get back to their camp with their friends and hopefully continue their deer hunt for a legitimate buck. I told them that if they came right out to the farm, I would work on the paperwork.

Within a half hour, the warden arrived with the two hunters and the two doe. I provided the paperwork, and they were able to pay their fine, sign a waiver, and put it in the mail, which took care of the immediate charges. I then took the game warden aside and said, "If possible, I would like to buy one of those deer to take to camp with me." It was a practice that game wardens would sell to "an appropriate person," a deer that had been killed either illegally or accidently with the revenue going back to the Fish and Game Department. As State's Attorney, I was "an appropriate person." The warden agreed, placed a metal tag in the ear of one deer, and it was legally mine.

At that time, I had an International Scout with four-wheel drive, which I was going to drive into the mountains to a deer camp owned by a friend of Gerry's, where we were invited guests. After loading the deer into the back of the Scout, I added my sleeping bag and duffle bag without realizing that one of the deer's back legs was visible through the back window. Gerry and I took off to Pittsfield for the camp. On the way, I stopped to refuel. I saw the attendant who was pumping gas glance at the Scout's rear window. He did not say a word and studiously looked away from both the window and me. I paid for the gas, and we were on our way, wondering what his thinking was but feeling quite confident that what he saw would remain with him alone. He would have had no idea that it was actually legal.

The camp was owned by Frank Lindholm and his brothers. Frank was a good friend of Gerry's and owned the Volkswagen franchise in Rutland. Gerry always drove a Volkswagen. Frank was Finnish and with his brothers he was also a part owner of Lindholm Sports—the leading outdoor sports store in Rutland.

The camp was very accommodating and more elaborate than one expects of a deer camp. The pride and joy of the camp was a Finnish sauna. When we arrived, Frank was there already but his brothers had not yet arrived. We explained to Frank about the deer and that I was glad to provide camp meat legally.

I had field dressed the deer before loading it into the truck and now that we were at camp, we hung it by its hind legs to a tree outside the camp. I then skinned one of its back legs and cut out some generous steaks from the leg to bring into the camp. Shortly, Frank's brothers arrived. They were thoroughly upset when they saw this doe hanging in their front yard. No matter how carefully I explained the story of how I obtained the deer and that it was perfectly legal for us to have it, they remained suspicious. I remained friends with Frank over the years, but I am not sure his brothers ever trusted me. In any case, I was never invited back to their camp.

One of the things I learned from that experience was that fresh-cut steaks from a carcass that was still partially warm were tough as hell. Since then I have always allowed any meat—whether it be deer or home-grown beef—to age properly.

Living on a farm all these years we have raised most of our meat. We actually have three freezers—one for beef, one for lamb, and one for pork. While I have always had a large vegetable garden and I love my vegetables, I am basically a carnivore at heart. While there are certainly more vegetarians today than when I started out my practice in 1960, most people I know still enjoy well-prepared quality meats.

When I hit my 60s it seemed that there were several local publications who wanted to do a feature story on my career. The University of Chicago magazine did an article entitled "The Road Less Taken." I got a call saying they would like to do a story about me if I was willing to be interviewed. This would also entail pictures of myself and family and farm. As a lawyer, I have always known that almost all publicity is good publicity, and I immediately accepted these requests.

The usual procedure was that the publications would have an independent writer or a staff person wanting to interview me and sometimes a separate photographer to document portions of the article photographically. They asked, "What would be a good time for an interview?" I suggested, "The best time to catch me is early in the morning. How about coming out to the farm for breakfast?" That way we would not be interrupted by phone calls or other distractions. They jumped at the chance. Over the years, Joann always got up early with me and made a cooked breakfast. It almost always included some form of meat—whether it be sausage, bacon, ham, a chop, a pork schnitzel, a small steak, or some fish or venison.

When our kids were growing up, breakfast was the one meal I could count on in having everybody together. The kids sometimes grumbled about not wanting that big breakfast but somehow managed to survive it and actually enjoy it. When the writers and photographers wanted to come out to the farm, it was almost routine to serve them a special breakfast. I found that serving lamb chops was always appreciated. After sitting down to a breakfast and informal conversation with the meal consisting of lamb chops, eggs, appropriate bread, and fresh fruit, it would set a tone that reverberated in the work they were doing. It was always a wonderful experience for me and I believe it was for them as well. It was not every day when doing a story that they were invited to sit down at a table and break bread with their interviewee and it consisted of home-grown lamb chops for breakfast.

CHAPTER 14
Alaska

In the early 1990s, I was involved as plaintiff's co-counsel in a class action in Sitka, Alaska. It involved the pollution of Silver Bay by the Japanese company, Alaska Pulp Company. The company had acquired a sweetheart contract with the United States to harvest Sitka Spruce from the Tongass National Forest. This was in the days when there was a policy to try to create jobs in Alaska to make it attractive for possible statehood. We had several persons interested in the environmental aspects of the case, but only one who was willing to risk having to answer to potentially devastating legal fees if we lost. Alaska's Rule 82 differs from most American law, where each side pays its own attorney. It instead follows the British Rule that makes the loser pay the winner's legal fees.

One person, Larry Edwards, was willing to risk it all, and he became the person representing the class of riparian owners that was eventually certified. At that time, the Defendant Alaska Pulp Company was controlled by one of Japan's "Big Four" financial houses. The Sitka operation was responsible for what was ranked as the fourth most serious pollution in the United States. The bay was so polluted with effluent from the mill that a clear white disk lost visibility in the first fathom of water.

The case lasted for several years and involved two trips to the Alaska Supreme Court, plus numerous court hearings in Sitka and Juneau. For three years, I was commuting from Middlebury, Vermont, to Sitka about every six weeks. It was a great adventure for me and brought me into contact with a lot of people with whom I both broke bread and shared libations.

During the course of the litigation, the company closed the mill and there were certain bars I dared not enter. These were frequented by mill workers who were upset with the mill closing, losing the high wages they had been earning. I believed that as we were considered carpetbaggers in bringing the action, those establishments were not safe venues for me. Fortunately, we had local counsel, a top Sitka lawyer by the name of James McGowan. We were also joined by Peter Einhardt, a partner in a law firm situated on the Kenai Peninsula. Einhardt not only participated in our case but was also one of the lead counsel in the plaintiff cases arising out of the Valdez oil spill.

Over time, I had many opportunities to break bread with both Jim and Peter. At one meal, I had the finest piece of fish I ever enjoyed. Jim suggested we drive out to a restaurant called The Channel House. The main road in Sitka leads nowhere in both directions. One way ended at the mill—about four miles east of town—and the other way was a short distance to the west. There is no way to drive to Sitka; all access to the city is either by plane or by boat. The particular restaurant, The Channel House, was located to the west of Sitka, and I had the good sense to order a fresh halibut filet. It was simply cooked on an open-flame grill and then topped with some melted butter. I had never had a piece of fish anywhere in the world that topped that evening's fare.

On another trip to Sitka, we had a retreat at a camp on a local river with the partners from Peter's firm, Jim McGowan, myself, and Terry Reed. Among the culinary treats we shared were generous portions of moose jerky.

We also took time off from the retreat to go fishing. Terry Reed, who was not a fisherman, was the only one to catch a salmon. We cooked that and it was great, but nothing compared to the halibut. On that fishing trip we carried a rifle in case we ran into an angry bear. Fortunately, we did not have to use it.

On another trip, I was seated on the airplane next to a commercial fisherman from Sitka. He had a boat and fished long lines for black cod, a fish that is caught at serious depths and requires great skill in setting the long line, all the while braving Alaska waters. We got talking about fishing. The plane was scheduled to stop in Ketchikan on the way to Sitka. The restaurant at the Ketchikan airport was famous for its pies. We deboarded and entered the airport where he introduced me to the tradition of having a piece of pie at Ketchikan while waiting for the plane to reload.

When we landed in Sitka, my new friend invited me to his home for dinner the following night. I readily accepted the invitation. On arrival at his house at 6:00 pm, I was greeted with a martini and, as an appetizer, some home-smoked salmon. For our first course, he provided cod cheeks, a delicacy, which was a new experience for me. For the main course, a haunch of venison. After dinner, he provided a homemade cordial, and we had a wide ranging conversation. In the course of the conversation, he asked me if I was a "liberal." I told him in fact that I was. He said he was glad to meet me as he had never met a "liberal" before (a different species for Alaskans). The next day, I had the bonus of visiting him at the docks and he showed me his boat which was in port at the time as the black cod fishing season had not yet opened. It was solidly built but looked a bit fragile for the cold water of the Alaskan Pacific.

Jim McGowan, our Alaskan co-council, was visiting family in the northeastern United States, and he made a detour to come and stay with us for a few days at the farm. Earlier in the week before he came, I had the good luck of finding a partridge (outside of season) that had been hit by a car but was still warm and relatively undamaged. I have no hesitancy in picking up a freshly killed partridge and taking it home to be properly hung and dressed. I served the bird to Jim and explained how I had obtained it. The next time I was in Alaska, the story of the partridge had been shared with his colleagues, and I took a great deal of kidding for serving Jim "roadkill."

I came close to the southern tip of Alaska on a trip with a friend George Dorsey to Prince Rupert, located in the northwest corner of British Columbia. We stayed over at a hotel in Vancouver, which had a bar that served high-quality martinis. More important than the martinis, perhaps, was the fact that they specialized in oysters on the half shell. While we were having our first martini, George ordered a large selection of west coast oysters. There are at least four different kinds of oysters that are grown on the west coast in the Pacific waters. He ordered a large platter that contained an ample number of each of the varieties. There were some oysters that I have never eaten before. There was one oyster that I had tasted in Europe, Belons. Belons were imported to be grown in the Pacific Ocean and are not usually grown on the east coast in the Atlantic. In fact, all mature Atlantic oysters from the Gulf of Mexico to Prince Edwards Island have the same genetic makeup. Their difference in size, salinity, and flavor is not based upon their genetics but upon the environment in which they live.

I am particularly partial to the northernmost range of the east coast oysters—especially the Malpeques that come from Prince Edward Island. They are smaller oysters grown in colder waters and have a distinctly gentle flavor and the right degree of salinity to suit my taste. While I enjoyed the variety of west coast oysters, I found that I still preferred the product of the Atlantic waters over those of the Pacific. If I had been raised on the west coast, my preference might be different.

CHAPTER 15

The Law Firm

I always believed from the very start of my practice that a serious lunch break was important. It divided the day in two, with a break in the middle where one could leave the morning's desk work behind and enjoy a wide-ranging discussion over lunch. It became a practice that all the lawyers in the office had lunch together every day.

In the early years, we almost always went to a local restaurant in town and sometimes lunch included libations. I had a rule that I never broke—I would not drink anything alcoholic before going into court (or before driving a horse). In most other situations, I was more flexible.

On one of our occasions at lunch, we went to the Waybury Inn in East Middlebury. The Waybury Inn is known widely as the front piece of Bob Newhart's show about a New England Inn and the local characters involved with it. One of our favorite libations at the inn we referred to as moose milk—in actuality a triple Brandy Alexander. One of these was enough to allow for a slow and relaxed luncheon.

Susan Humphrey was an associate, a graduate of Shimer College and Northeastern School of Law, and a truly fine lawyer. At lunch one day with my then partner Fred Parker, Susan ordered a hamburger. The hamburger was served on slices of homemade bread rather than a roll. It was cut in half. Susan ate one half of the hamburger and left the other on the plate. Fred and I, both being raised at the end of the Great Depression, were trained not to leave anything on our plate. We kidded her about not finishing her hamburger. She then said something that I will never forget. "I am an adult and one of the things about being an adult is you can make your own decisions. I decide what I'm going to eat and not the restaurant." I have always remembered that statement, and, while I never quite live up to it, I certainly, on many occasions, remind myself of her thoughts. Her statement challenging the two senior partners played a positive part in her early invitation to become a partner in the firm.

The tradition of all the lawyers having lunch together every day continues to this very day. However, we do not go to restaurants as often but rather order out sandwiches and then join each other in a conference room. The lawyers in the firm are fortunate enough to like each other and enjoy each other's company. The luncheon discussions range from evaluating cases and telling stories about what they are presently involved in to discussing hockey and whether the Boston Red Sox will recover from their present slump.

One of the benefits of having a firm lunch was that oftentimes a visiting dignitary or a lawyer from out of town would join us, often igniting a more ranging discussion. It was also invaluable in recruiting young lawyers and making them realize that our firm was a place that valued the breaking of bread together as an important part of the firm culture.

The luncheon part of the culture of our law firm mirrors the French. In 1894 the French government issued a decree that barred eating lunch at the workplace. This was originally issued as a health order as the workplaces were often unsanitary and lunchtime was a time when the owners used to air out work buildings and clean out much of the odor and sometimes dangerous materials that accumulated in the manufacturing process. This practice, however, soon turned into a cultural icon. Martin Bruegel, an expert on French culinary traditions, stated, "The separation between work and lunch is almost sacrosanct." This lunch break usually lasts for ninety minutes. That often includes a visit to a bistro and perhaps a glass or two of wine. Bruegel goes on to say that people are simply happier when they have some downtime during the workday. I totally agree with this, and I think my joy in continuing to practice law has, in part, depended upon socialization and the discussions that take place at our daily firm lunches. It is a wonderful time to work out conflicts and to come to understand the persons you work with.

Unfortunately, Covid brought this practice in our firm to a complete halt because people were working remotely and for a long time were prevented from meeting face to face—either with clients or with other members of the firm. This also happened in France, where a legal ban of eating at the desk was suspended because of Covid. As Covid receded, this resulted in an attempt to repeal the 1894 decree. Thankfully, the French had the good sense of preventing that from happening, and as Covid winds down, the tradition of the lunch break in France is returning to its pre-Covid level.

In our law firm, our daily firm lunches returned; however, it has not reached the pre-Covid level because of changed work habits, as many lawyers and staff continue doing some work remotely. There is another factor working that tends to diminish this important tradition. The information revolution has brought about so many technical changes that diminish the opportunity for people to talk to each other face to face. These changes have put additional pressures in terms of billing time and the increased expectation of more rapid responses, all making it less convenient to gather together to break bread at lunch. While the tradition has not vanished, it has diminished. Hopefully, it will be recaptured to its original status, thus extending the tremendous benefits that occur when people sit down and talk over things—business or otherwise—while having lunch.

Breaking bread has always been important after partnership meetings. We have a rule that before a partnership meeting, no one is going to drink, even though the partnership meetings are often at cocktail hour. However, after the partnership meetings, we often go to a restaurant to share food, libations, and conversations.

There was one dinner meeting with the partners and two associates that was special. In the mid-1970s there were not many female members of the Vermont bar. From the beginning of the republic of Vermont in 1777, through its statehood in 1791, and for 200 years, there had been less than seventy women who had been admitted to the bar. Most of them were working with spouses and, with only a few exceptions, women were not involved in litigation. In the mid 1970s, the firm consisted of four male lawyers: Mark Sperry, Fred Parker, John Stahl, and myself. We had been raised in a chauvinist tradition but were trying to learn our way out of it. We needed to take on an additional associate, and we were looking specifically for a woman. We had two top-flight candidates. Susan Humphrey, who came to us as an intern law clerk for a spring quarter and again for the fall quarter of her final year under the co-op program at Northeastern Law School. During the summer, Ellen Fallon, a law student at the University of Pennsylvania, was our summer law clerk. Both were highly qualified persons, and it appeared that both were anxious for us to make them an offer. In December, we were to make a decision about giving either of them an offer. We were faced with a dilemma. Susan was working with us through that period of time and was present. Ellen, on the other hand, was back at Penn. She kept us advised of her continued interest in joining the firm by regularly sending little tidbits of law about cases she had been familiar with while working in the summer. This reminded us that she was still around and wanted to be considered for a permanent job.

We had a partnership meeting, and the four of us decided we should offer both of them jobs and we would be able to find enough work to keep them both busy. It turned out to be a very good decision. Not only did the two of them prove themselves capable beyond expectation, but we had two women with different personalities and individual agendas, creating a critical mass to interact with the traditional chauvinism.

This decision played a role in my becoming friends with Hillary Clinton. Hillary was chair of the American Bar Association Committee on the Status of Women in the Legal Profession. I testified before that committee and told them how important it was to have a critical mass of women as lawyers as it prevented them from being singled-out as an oddity. When we made this move, we were concerned that some of our clients might not be satisfied to have a woman as an attorney. We decided if that was the case, the clients could go, and if they didn't like who was assigned to the case, that was their prerogative. It turned out that never happened. One more mark for our growing out of our chauvinistic approach. Hillary appreciated our firm's position, and my testimony and this appearance was the start of a continuing friendship.

The importance of this decision also played out in future years as we were able to recruit some of the finest female legal minds in the country. Susan Murray and Beth Robinson were among those recruits. They took on, with the firm's blessing, the task of securing the rights of gay people to marry. They were extraordinarily successful in that they worked together, prepared, and, with Beth's brilliant argument before the Vermont Supreme Court, accomplished the creation of the first recognition of those rights: Baker vs

Vermont. As a result, the Vermont legislature passed a civil union bill giving gay couples the same rights as married couples.

They, however, went even further and finally convinced the Vermont legislature to change the civil union into a full marriage. In order to do this, they had to eventually organize and override the Governor's veto. They accomplished this by extensive contact with individual legislators, winning the override by a single vote. Unfortunately for the firm but not for the country, Beth left us first to be counsel to the governor, then a justice of the Vermont Supreme Court, and is now a judge on the United States Court of Appeals for the Second Circuit. I am proud of the firm, which backed our partners in their pursuit of justice to the extent of approving one million dollars of time while keeping them at full compensation. Beth was selected by *The Burlington Free Press* as the Vermonter of the year for the year 2000. Susan, Beth, and I were also selected as civil rights heroes by the *Human Rights Magazine* of the American Bar Association. The *National Law Journal* also selected our firm as the pro bono firm of the year for 2000 over any other firm in the United States.

Emily Joselson, another partner, has developed a national reputation as a plaintiff's environmental lawyer, always wearing the white hat. In the course of her practice, she took time to write two scholarly Law Review articles where, not surprisingly, her underlying arguments were adopted by the Vermont Supreme Court.

I could share the talents of the other women in our firm and it would be a book in itself, but it is fair to say that women have a full presence within the firm, equitably and numerically.

But back to the special dinner. Both Susan Humphrey and Ellen Fallon were doing such high-quality work that the four male partners agreed "there is no reason why we have to wait to make them partners." And so, only two and a half years out of law school, we voted to invite them into the partnership. We arranged for a dinner at The Common Man in Waitsfield, a top-drawer restaurant, to announce our decision to them. Fred's wife, Barbie, made carefully hand-crafted scrolls of the offer to them, which were rolled and then tied with a ribbon. We all arrived at The Common Man without anything being said. Susan and Ellen had no idea what was up and certainly they had not really contemplated an offer of partnership. They were more concerned about possible other things that might happen in a law firm. As we sat down, Fred handed each of the women one of the scrolls. They opened them, and the response was emotional. There was no question that they accepted the invitation, and that night the libations were champagne rather than martinis. As a footnote, they were the first two women admitted into a firm as full litigation partners in Vermont's history.

Merritt Chandler, a friend of the firm, was the head of Xerox Operations in Europe. When he retired, he settled in Middlebury and for a summer home bought an island in the middle of Lake Bomoseen, twenty-five miles southwest of Middlebury. This was the island that had formed the summer playground for the infamous Algonquin Club, which included the likes of Groucho Marks and Dorothy Parker. By the time he purchased the island, it had long been vacated by the New York celebrities. Retirement did not sit particularly well with Merritt. While he had no need to return to the pressures of international business, he wanted something interesting to do that was both meaningful and kept him busy.

He took a job as business manager for the Addison County Supervisory Union District. In his job, occasionally minor problems with potential legal consequences arose, and he was reluctant to incur legal costs to deal with matters that he felt were his responsibility to handle. He solved the problem by giving me a call. His questions about school business never required a formal opinion but were answered in the nature of friendly advice, combining some knowledge of law and some knowledge of the community. Our discussions always took place at about 5:00 pm when he would arrive at the office with a bottle of scotch in hand. The scotch was from the Perth Single Malt Society in Perth, Scotland. This whisky was taken straight from the original barrels without blending or adulteration of any kind. Each bottle was labeled with data concerning the original cask and its alcohol percentage that sometimes reached 120 proof. They were unique single malts and of exceptionally high quality. We would open the bottle and have a drink or two. He would then insist upon leaving the remains of the bottle for me. This was my fee for giving him the casual advice that he sought. Our conversations over these unique scotches often ranged far beyond his immediate questions. It was delightful to share thoughts and libations with such an intelligent and well-traveled person.

At the time of his second retirement—this time from the school district—he gave me a gift membership to the Perth Single Malt Society. The membership included two bottles of scotch whisky and four specially engraved glasses from the society. After consuming the two bottles, I inquired about purchasing more whisky as a member. I was certainly welcome to do so. The recognition that each bottle would cost in the neighborhood of $125 was a bit daunting. I explained it to Joann, and she said, "If Merritt Chandler thinks you should drink hundred-and-twenty-five-dollar bottles of scotch, perhaps you should." For a period of time, I occasionally splurged and bought a bottle. Eventually my cost/benefit analysis ingrained in me from days at the University of Chicago and my exposure to Milton Friedman, eventually ended that process. However, the glasses are still on the mantlepiece of my office fireplace, and I often use them when friends or clients join me for a late afternoon libation.

Sometimes the sharing of a beverage under friendly conditions leads to a surprising result. For twenty years, Fred Parker and I were partners. Fred and I were both born on the same day—Groundhog Day, 1938. We never asked what time of day we were born because we did not want to establish seniority. Fred left the partnership to become a federal judge and ended up being one of only six Vermonters ever appointed to the Second Circuit Court of Appeals. One other of those six was Beth Robinson, who is now sitting on the Court.

Each year, Fred and I would take a weekend off in late November or early December for a mini retreat to analyze how the previous year had gone and what approaches we would take in the following year. We acted, in effect, as a two-person compensation committee. Our goal was to treat everyone fairly and to stay away from an eat-what-you-kill philosophy that we felt created internal competition in the firm that was potentially destructive.

One year, our mini retreat took us to the Lake Placid Club in Lake Placid, New York. It is a marvelous venue and is the site of two winter Olympics and usually has a great deal of activity. However, this time it was in late November, there was no snow, and Lake Placid was basically dead. After dinner, we took a walk from the Lake Placid Club towards the Holiday Inn in hopes of finding a bar where there was some activity going on. In our walk through Lake Placid, we observed three people coming from the other direction. We figured out they were three people staying at the Holiday Inn that were coming to the Lake Placid Club with the same thoughts we had in mind.

Nothing was happening at the Holiday Inn, so we took a walk through town. We walked by a small local bar that seemed to have a reasonable number of people in it and a pool table. We decided to have a beer and a game of pool. The pool table was not in use, and after Fred and I chose our pool cues and were ready to start a game of eight ball, two young men asked if they could join us for a game. We were happy to have friendly company and welcomed them. One of them suggested that we should have a small wager. Fred and I were not pool sharks, but they only suggested a wager of a round of beers. We were okay being hustled to that level and agreed. In the middle of the game, one of our new friends made a scratch. The way he hit the ball it looked to me as if the scratch was deliberate. He happily bought us a round of beers and said let's play another game for the same stakes.

We could hardly refuse and agreed. Shortly into the game while Fred was shooting, one of them said to me, "Can I do some work for you?" I replied, "What do you mean?" He said, "Well I can do anything—I can help make trips for you or make deliveries or anything you might need." I immediately put two and two together and came up with four. I said to Fred "Fred, I think we found ourselves a couple of narcs!" Our two friends vanished into the woodwork and never finished the game or their beers. Unfortunately, Fred died at a relatively young age while still active on the Second Circuit. I recounted the story at Fred's memorial before the entire circuit court bench. I started my comments by saying that I had never appeared in the circuit before en banc (meaning all the judges at once rather than a three-judge panel) but it was not for want of trying. I then explained to them how their former colleague had been mistaken in Lake Placid as a potential drug dealer.

All of our mini retreats over the years involved a fun venue and a good meal. Memorable was the time we went to Montreal and had dinner at Les Halles, a top French restaurant. We spent about three hours at dinner, starting with cocktails, a foie gras appetizer, a good steak with pommes frites, and then dessert followed by coffee and eau de vies. After finishing the dinner, we walked out onto Pell Street, and Fred looked at me and said, "You know, we're close to Ben's right around the corner. Maybe we should have a Montreal smoked meat sandwich to finish the evening." Ben's specialty. We did just that.

CHAPTER 16

Wild Turkeys

When Vermont was first settled, the environment supported wild turkeys. As 80% of Vermont's forested lands were cleared for farming, much of it subsistence farms, the wild turkeys disappeared. In the last century, much of Vermont's subsistence farms, especially those in the hillier country, were abandoned and the fields that had been cleared returned to forest.

In the 1960s, the Vermont Department of Fish and Game reintroduced wild turkeys. Since then, turkeys have flourished and now seem to be everywhere. On the one hand, it is considered a success in that it has opened up a whole new avenue of big-game hunting. Turkeys are treated as big game, much as moose, deer or bear are considered. There is another side. In the early summer, after they have hatched, you will sometimes see as many as forty birds walking through a field in a straight line, much as an army would. God help any grasshoppers that are in front of them. Unfortunately, grasshoppers are not the only item on their menus. They will eat anything, including the eggs of ground-nesting birds, such as whip-poor-wills or ruffed grouse.

On our farm, as the turkeys came, the evening song of the whippoorwill disappeared. I think they have also had a tremendous effect on the grouse, which were once plentiful in my area but now are seldom seen. Despite my frustration at those birds' disappearance, I have joined the throng of turkey hunters.

When a turkey is killed, it should be field dressed immediately. Partridge, woodcock, and pheasant should all be hung without being dressed for several days. The guts remaining in the bird while they are hanging do not affect their table potential except in a positive way. On the other hand, a turkey left hanging with its guts inside may very well spoil.

On my front porch, I have nails along the upper board near the outside end of the porch. This is where I hang my birds before plucking, gutting, and getting them ready for the table. The same porch, which serves as our main visiting area during the summer, is also used to store firewood starting in the fall and running through the winter. I once shot a young turkey—about nine pounds—field dressed it and hung it from one of the nails. What I had not paid any attention to was that I had hung it close to the woodpile. Two days later, I returned from the office with the expectation of finishing my job by plucking it and getting it ready for the table. When I arrived home, it was missing. I asked Joann what happened, and she said, "Bill, one of our English setters, managed to get up on the wood pile and take down the turkey. He wandered off with it in his mouth, head hanging out one side and the tail feathers on the other side." Joann said that she'd tried to entice him to bring it back, but he was off in the woods to stow it somewhere for future use. The DNA of wolves seems to remain strong in the English setter. I talked to Bill and tried to have him take me to where he had hid it. I was not successful.

The next day, when I returned home, Joann said Bill had found the turkey and was parading it in his mouth back and forth in front of the house. I said, "Did you try to get it away from him?" and she just laughed. I have been more careful in hanging birds from the rafter ever since.

We have several flocks of turkeys on the home farm. In the spring, it is not unusual for us to see individual flocks of twelve turkeys or more counting the hen and ten to twelve chicks working their way through a pasture. Sometimes the flocks combine and you will see as many as forty, including three or four hens and the rest chicks.

Sometimes the big toms group together—often showing off in full display. One year we had four large toms, each in the twenty-pound class with beards almost a foot long. In full display, each tom would fluff out his feathers and spread his tail like a wide-open fan with his beard bouncing from his chest. When a tom is not displaying, it is best to tell him apart from a hen by the fact that he has a beard that consists of horsehair like hairs standing out in a tassel from the upper part of his breast.

The wild turkeys on our farm have become almost tame. This is probably because there are leftover bits of grain from where we feed the sheep, beef cattle, and horses. We often have turkeys visiting our bird feeder not twenty-five feet from the house, challenging the songbirds for grain that has spilled out from the feeders. (Yes, we do keep bird feeders out year round despite the occasional foray of a black bear coming off the mountain.)

There are two turkey seasons—one in the spring where you can kill only toms, and one in the fall where you take either a hen or a tom. The two seasons present different challenges. In the spring, the turkeys are likely to be scattered and the chicks kept under close supervision by the mother hen. This is when a hunter goes out to an area where he believes there are turkeys roosting nightly in a particular stand of trees, coming down to the ground in the morning. The hunter tries to call the turkeys, staying motionless, camouflaged, and in a position where his or her outline is well hidden. There are all sorts of turkey calls that are used. Mine is a device scratching a piece of slate that mimics the sound of a turkey.

One year I received a report from a farmer friend that there were a flock of turkeys in a wood lot on his farm. The next morning I got up early and, just before dawn, went out into the woods and found myself a large pine tree. Turkeys have sufficient eyesight so when you call them—or try to call them—you want to be in a position where it is difficult for them to make you out, either by way of silhouette or any perceived movement. I settled myself down in a niche at the roots of the tree with my shotgun across my lap and my little slate box in my hands. As dawn started to break, I noted movement about 200 yards away that looked like it might be a turkey coming out of a tree off the roost to the ground. I used my slate to try and call it. About ten minutes later, I heard a rustling coming towards me from behind the tree. I convinced myself that there was a tom turkey making its way towards the hen turkey I was trying to imitate. I waited until the rustling of the leaves behind me was clearly within potential range, and I stood up and turned around ready to shoot a turkey. Instead, there were two large coyotes running hell-bent for leather towards where I was sitting. They saw me, button hook turned, and disappeared before I could get a shot at them. It was then I became convinced that my calling skills were limited to making the sounds of a sick turkey.

Fall season starts on the third Saturday in October, and each year I and my farm manager wait with anticipation for opening day with the hopes of harvesting one of the turkeys that we had been feeding all summer. Almost like clockwork, two days before the season, the turkeys disappear. I do not think they can read a calendar, but it sure seems like it. They actually retreat up to higher grounds to gather the acorns and other mast that have fallen from the trees. Occasionally, however, some turkeys cannot give up the easy picking around the farmyard. I had the chance to harvest one when the flock appeared within fifty feet of my barn. That same year my farm manager, Matt, harvested a turkey. It was the day before the sixteen-day season was coming to a close and Matt was at the back side of the barn near our chicken runs. Our chickens have a wired-in run, and in good weather we let them out to peck throughout the whole farmyard. On this occasion, a door to one of the pens was open and as Matt came around the corner of the barn, he saw a turkey making its way across the front of the chicken run with the open door. He picked up a stick and tried to hit it. The panicked turkey ran into the chicken run. Matt went in after it, but the turkey managed to get back to the door and started to fly away. Matt grabbed a hayfork that was standing near the door of the coop and threw it at the turkey like a spear. Unbelievably, he managed to hit it and bring it down. He then was able to retrieve the turkey, and he had his turkey for the fall turkey season. When he told me the story with words and gestures, I could not help but ask him, "What gauge pitchfork did you use?" This all gave new meaning to the word 'pitchfork'.

This was a one-up on Matt's father. His father, nicknamed Tiny because he was not tiny, was my farm manager before Matt took over upon his dad's death. Tiny came to work for me when he was seventy-six years old, and he had five teenage boys and a wife to support. One of the sons, Matt's brother, George, was intent upon becoming a turkey hunter. He bought himself a camouflaged shotgun, camouflaged clothes, and went out to hunt turkeys early in the morning on opening day. He came back later that morning without having seen a turkey. Tiny said to him, "Go look in the back of the house—I got a turkey earlier today." George thought he was being put on but went to check and found a turkey hanging from a beam. Tiny, when going out to feed the sheep, had run across a turkey that was hiding in some tall grass in the pasture. He'd reached down and grabbed a stick, hit it over its head, and brought it back for the Thanksgiving Day dinner. George was chagrined. That story soon became a part of the lore of turkey hunting on our farm. Matt's spear throwing seemed to top that, but not by much.

One of the pleasures of fall turkey hunting for me was that I could hunt grouse and woodcock with my English setters in areas where we would sometimes run into a flock of turkeys. The dogs would run into the flock and chase them. The turkeys, seeing the dog coming, would leave the ground and land in nearby trees. The dogs, frustrated in not being able to catch up with the turkeys, would see them in the tree, go under the tree, and start barking. This all being reminiscent of a hound treeing a racoon or a bear and then barking. I could hear the commotion and the barking and realized what happened. It was a relatively easy matter to trace down the dogs by their bark. I would arrive at the tree and be able to harvest a turkey from the tree they were barking at.

One evening, during the fall season, I was getting dressed to go out for dinner when I looked out the bedroom window and saw a flock of ten turkeys working on the far side of the north pasture. I immediately abandoned my evening clothes, put on a pair of boots, grabbed my shotgun, hopped into the pickup truck, and drove into the pasture. The turkeys were not afraid of the truck, and I was able to get reasonably close. I got out of the truck on the far side from them and came around. At this point, they had realized that the truck contained a human being and started heading towards the woods. I managed to shoot the last one before it got into the woods. I took it back to the house, field-dressed it, hung it, went in, washed up, got dressed, and we were only five minutes late to the dinner party.

Bill Rule and I were hunting partridges one day with my English setter Ella. We hunted through a second growth forest area and were coming out to an overgrown meadow. In the meadow, there was a scattering of stunted juniper bushes scattered through the tall grass. Suddenly in front of me Ella came to a point. It was not, however, her usual point as her tail was not out straight but was wavering. I walked up behind her. "Ella, have you got a damned rabbit in there?" I gestured toward the juniper bush. Just as I spoke, the bush exploded and a large tom turkey took off. I was so excited that I fired my first shot right in the air and missed the turkey. My second shot, however, brought it down about twenty-five yards in front of me. Before I could say a word, Ella was on top of it, holding its wings down to make sure it would not get away and started plucking it. It turned out to be a twenty-two-pound tom turkey—the biggest I ever shot.

Enough about harvesting turkeys, though each turkey that is harvested seems to come with its own story. Let's talk about the joy of a wild turkey at table. Each bird that I kill I treat with great respect. I carefully dry-pluck it so that it can be roasted whole. It takes some time as there are a lot of feathers. The tailfeathers I usually save for a reason I do not know exactly why but probably traces back to my childhood. I have harvested turkeys that weigh between seven and fifteen pounds when dressed. They look much like a domestic turkey, although their breasts are not quite so full and sometimes the skin is broken by a shotgun pellet. I stuff it and cook it as I would a domestic turkey. I roast it breast down and then turn it over to let it brown before taking it out of the oven. It comes out tender with a moist breast, which to my taste has more flavor than a domestic turkey. At the end of the meal, I save the carcass and make a wild turkey stock, add some vegetables, and, in keeping with the theme, I throw in some wild rice and have a wonderful wild turkey soup. There is something special that goes beyond the taste about having a wild turkey for Thanksgiving and sharing it with friends.

My dear friend and a uniform law colleague, Miller Rudd, and his wife, Barbara, came from Washington D.C. to join us for Thanksgiving. We shared a wild turkey together. We also opened a bottle of wine I had saved especially for sharing with Millard, a wine connoisseur: a Mouton Rothchild (1971).

It was a dinner a bit more sophisticated than what the Pilgrims shared with the Indians in the first Thanksgiving, but one which made me feel a part of the continuation of the natural order of things.

CHAPTER 17

Fishing

Bill Rule, my closest hunting and fishing partner and Stan Lawrence, a patent attorney from New York City, went on a trip to Labrador to fish for Arctic char. We flew commercially to Gander and then flew in a de Havilland Beaver to the fishing camp. On our first day of fishing, the three of us climbed into our third plane, a single engine Cessna float plane, and flew about forty miles north into a section of a river that flattened out and looked like a lake. On route, I was sitting in the co-pilot seat—a seat without dual controls in front of me. In looking at the instrument panel, I discovered there were all holes; there was not a single instrument of significance in the panel. I thought, "Oh what the hell, I'm sure the pilot with many years of flying in the bush knows exactly what he is doing." Fortunately, he did. I did have some second doubts when, after we landed on the river, he reached behind his seat, took out a quart of oil, walked out on the pontoon, and poured it into the engine.

We were wearing waders and fishing from near the shore. The pilot was also our guide. He suggested that we cast a spoon out near the channel of the river. On the first cast, Bill brought back a seven-pound char. Our guide took out of his jacket a pair of pliers and commanded, "Squeeze down all the barbs on your lures as you are going to catch a lot of fish, and this will make releasing them a lot easier—both on ourselves and on the fish." We caught a lot of fish. At noon we stopped for lunch. Our pilot was also our cook. He expertly fileted two nice char and took a large frying pan from behind the back seat on the plane and cooked them over a wood fire. The fire was built along a stretch of beach alongside the river. Sharing a fresh filet of char that had not been out of the river more than a few minutes before it hit the frying pan is a culinary treat reserved for fisher persons. Of course, it was accompanied by some beer that we somehow had managed to fit into the plane for the trip.

This beautiful Labrador day, I shared the food with others than just my fishing companions. After lunch I worked myself in my waders out about fifty feet from shore into some shallow water that got about three feet deep yet close enough to the main channel of the river that I could cast into it. I was kept busy catching fish. Using a fly rod and a large streamer fly, I brought nineteen fish to the net each about five pounds. Suddenly something attracted my eye towards the beach, where a few minutes before we had enjoyed our lunch. One hundred yards downstream, a large black bear had decided to come to join us for lunch. The bear decided to finish off the char carcasses that we'd left near our luncheon spot. The bear looked at me but appeared to take little notice. I was aware that black bears generally are not dangerous to humans, but being within one hundred yards of one and totally exposed in the middle of a river, I hoped this animal was not an exception. After the bear finished eating the carcasses, he took a look at me, proceeded to hump his back then take a dump and wander back into the bush. Shortly after this, we quitted the river, got back in the instrumentless Cessna, took off upstream into the wind, and made a large circle, looking for a herd of caribou before we turned around and headed back to the camp. Thus, the sharing of food without sharing libations.

There must be an undiscovered generic trait that is passed on somehow so that a select number of people are born with it and that is the gene to become a fisherperson. I have gone on a lot of fishing trips over the course of my life, and an integral part of all of them involve breaking bread and drinking martinis or an appropriate substitute.

One year I took my eldest son, Fritz, a law partner, on a trip salmon fishing to Newfoundland. We were fly fishing for Atlantic salmon, the king of all sports fish. We stayed in a lodge in the town of St. Anthony and were provided with a local guide to help us search out the elusive salmon. We were both successful in landing some salmon, but more than once we experienced what is known as a long-distance release when the salmon decided—after playing with you on the rod for a while—to shake off the fly and take off on his own, not coming to the net.

Newfoundland abounds in moose. They are everywhere. The hunting rate of success is about 90%, and you can stop at restaurants along the highway and obtain a mooseburger. One night after dinner, our fishing guide suggested he would take us on a ride in the area and we saw twenty-four moose, including six bulls—the bulls all together and sporting large racks.

The next day after fishing in the morning, our guide invited us to take a trip on a boat owned by his brother-in-law to see the area from the water. We readily accepted, and we explored the northern tip of Newfoundland and some of its many bays. As we motored into a deep bay, our guide smiled at his brother and said, "This looks like a good place." His brother turned to Fritz and myself, "Do you guys like mussels?" We said, "Of course." He then pulled the boat near the shore of the bay, threw out an anchor, and we waded to the shore. He unloaded a small steamer equipped with a propane tank and set it up on shore. He suggested we walk out into the shallow water among the seaweed beds where we would find beds of mussels. We followed his suggestion, and in the clear shallow water we gathered a couple of pecks of mussels. Upon bringing them back to shore, they were immediately steamed and consumed au natural. The appropriate accompaniment was Molson's Canadian. A treat that is hard to duplicate.

On that trip, we also became honorary Newfoundlanders. There are three requirements for becoming one. First, you have to speak a full sentence of the Newfoundland language. Second, you have to kiss the cod, and third you must partake of some screech.

What they refer to as the Newfoundland language is actually English but spoken extremely rapidly and over a monotone pitch with no punctuation. If you were to say, "The fishing today was very good," it would look like THEFISHINGTODAYWASVERYGOOD and said in half the time. It can be done but it is not easy, and it always involves laughter at those performing the ceremony. The second requirement of kissing a cod is much harder than it was some years earlier. Cod fishing in this area, which had been the backbone of this local economy, was no longer allowed because overfishing had destroyed the stock. However, our host had managed to find a cod and have it frozen. The frozen cod was brought out and presented, and the kissing of a frozen fish was obviously not difficult. Again, this was accompanied by joyous laughter and many various comments about the kissing. Partaking screech was the easiest of all. Newfoundland was part of the trade route that sent dried salted cod fish to England and the rest of the world and received, from the British West Indies, strong rum made from cane sugar. Screech is a heavy-duty rum and poured liberally was used for several toasts as we were initiated as honorary Newfoundlanders.

Part of our trip involved taking a converted fishing boat through "iceberg alley," a regular tourist attraction. After seeing many icebergs and realizing that 90% of its bulk remained under water and seeing many whales, we were invited to have a glass of screech. The deckhand with a long-handled net worked over the side of the boat and retrieved a piece of ice broken off one of the icebergs. Then, with an ice pick, he broke it up into smaller pieces, placing them in a plastic cup. Screech was then poured over the ice, and you could hear it crackling as it expanded from its 15,000 years of pressure.

I have always enjoyed old whiskey poured over new ice, but this was the first time I experienced new whiskey over old ice.

In 1967, when I was first appointed to the Uniform Law Conference, the meeting was held in Hawaii. Joann had lived in Honolulu as a child. In fact, she was there on December 7, 1941, and some of her first memories are of hearing planes dropping bombs. Fortunately, her father, who was a submarine commander, was out to sea and was not involved in the devastation that occurred at Pearl Harbor. We dropped our two young children off in San Diego in the care of Joann's parents, where they lived after her father's retirement from the navy at the rank of Admiral, and continued on to Hawaii.

We had scheduled a trip after the meeting to fish for marlin. It was not successful. Through four days, we did not have a single strike. Between the sun and the diesel fumes and Joann's and my tendency towards seasickness, it is not a trip that, as much as I like fishing, I plan to repeat.

One memory from the Hawaiian trip was a truly pleasant surprise. On our first morning, I went to breakfast with Joann. It was a buffet breakfast and featured on the buffet were large chunks of fresh pineapple. I had always loved pineapple, but what I tasted in Hawaii was like nothing I was familiar with. It was field ripened, sweet, and so flavorful that it was miles ahead of what I experienced in buying pineapples in Vermont. I must admit that I could not resist it, and while I may have had something else from the buffet,

I know I ate a prodigious amount of pineapple. In fact, I ate so much its acidity caused what seemed like canker sores in my mouth. I soon recovered and continued to eat pineapple while I was there, but in more moderate quantities.

Another culinary experience we had in Hawaii was that we found a small steakhouse. They served a simple house steak, artichokes, and a baked potato. I do not think they had anything else on the menu. The efficiency of such a limited menu allowed the pricing to be extremely attractive and the service prompt. If I were ever to open a restaurant, that would be one to model it after.

I have had an image of a restaurant that was a take-off on their simple menu approach and that was to open a restaurant where the only item on the menu was a planked stuffed salmon. It would be baked whole, with a saltine, onion, and caper stuffing, and then served at the table. When baked on a plank, the skin on top pulls away, leaving the flesh untouched. The filets can be pulled away with a serving spatula. Next, the whole bone can be removed in one piece, exposing the other side for further serving. On the plate, it would be drenched with butter laced with a little lemon juice. It would be accompanied by a simple vegetable like sautéed spinach or a lettuce salad. I think the concept might work, but you would need a population center and certainly nothing that could be dealt with in rural Vermont. While I still serve salmon this way at home, I decided to stick to lawyering.

My grandson, Peter, and I were in Winnipeg, the launching pad for a Northwest Territories fishing trip. We went out to dine in a high-class Italian restaurant. The waiter brought the wine list, and I handed it to Peter. I wanted him to select the wine for the night.

While on a few occasions I have had a chance to taste wines from some of the world's best vineyards, most times I am presented with a menu of wines that I know nothing about. Quite frankly, I have never been able to fully understand the descriptions written extolling the virtues of any particular wine. A taste of cherry or black currant with a somewhat fruity aftertaste and the like has never translated to my palette when drinking the wine. I can tell a really good wine from a mediocre or bad wine, but my palette is not sophisticated enough to make any meaningful decisions beyond that level.

I suggested to my grandson that some night he would be out on a date wanting to order a bottle of wine, and I expected him to be in the same situation I was where he had very little knowledge about the individual wines on the menu. I suggested to him that if he was trying to impress his date, he should probably not select the cheapest wine on the menu but order a wine that was somewhere at the lower end of the price range. Following my advice, he looked over the menu and decided on an Italian wine that was selling for $45 a bottle, about $4 more than the least expensive wine on the list. The waiter came over, Peter named the wine he wanted, and the waiter said, "A very good choice." What Peter hadn't noticed was that wine with the same name but of a higher quality was also on the wine list at $115. The wine arrived, we tasted it, and it was certainly of a high quality, and we were very pleased. At the end of the meal, I was presented with the bill and saw that the wine we had drank was the $115 bottle. I called the waiter over and said there must be some mistake, we had ordered the $45 bottle of wine from the same vineyard. The waiter apologized for the mistake and said he would charge us one-half the listed price for the $115 bottle or $62.50. It was a reasonable compromise, and I paid the substantial bill but with a $62.50 reduction. Everybody was happy.

The result, of course, was that Peter could brag that when he went to dinner with his grandfather in Winnipeg, his grandfather had allowed him to order a $115 bottle of wine. That was more than I had ever paid for a bottle of wine for myself. I don't know how often he has told the story, but it gave him some unusual bragging rights.

CHAPTER 18

Family and Friends

My best friend is my wife, Joann, and over the years we have shared many meals between just the two of us. As we are in our late 80s, we often reminisce about those meals, recognizing the role they have played in our 65+ years of marriage. On our trips to Europe, we have often splurged to have a meal in one of Europe's top restaurants.

On a family trip to Lyon, France, we made a reservation for the two of us at the world-renowned restaurant of chef Paul Bocuse. Not only was the food fantastic, but the décor was equally sensational. The color of the roses on the table matched the cream-colored walls of the restaurant itself. We ordered a roast chicken served in a parchment bag. Its presentation was a first for both of us. The presentation matched the magnificent food.

We had left our children at the hotel so that we could enjoy this special meal together. At the end of the meal, they served an assortment of petit fours. We had eaten well and then thought somewhat guilty of our children at the hotel and decided to take the petit fours home to them. I placed them in a tissue and into my pocket. As I was doing so, a waiter noticed me slipping something into my pocket and apparently was concerned that we were trying to take a piece of silverware with us as a souvenir. Of course we had no intention of doing that. The waiter kept an eye on us as we walked out of the restaurant to the parking lot and our car. I am sure they were relieved when they counted the silverware and realized that we had taken nothing of value as a souvenir.

On a trip to Paris, we splurged to have a luncheon at Tour d'Argent. Experience has taught us that you can get the same quality food at a luncheon that you can at dinner, but at a lower price. Tour d'Argent is on the second floor of a building with windows that open onto a view of the backside of Notre Dame Cathedral. Their specialty is duck. When you order a duck, which is for two persons, they present a dressed duck that is raised especially for them, bearing an identifying number. We approved the duck, and it was then taken away to be served in three separate courses. The last course involved pressing a portion of the duck, which is done with a unique kitchen press, on a trolley that was moved to our table for the waiter to perform his specialized skills.

We ordered a good bottle of wine but nowhere near the top shelf. Their wine list is the most extensive that I had ever seen, with some bottles running into thousands of dollars. The history of their wine list includes its survival during the Nazi occupation of Paris. The best of their wines were hidden behind a newly constructed brick wall in their wine cellar and that wall was not demolished until after the liberation of Paris. We did not take petit fours on that occasion, nor did we take any silverware as a souvenir. Tour d'Argent had the wise policy of giving each guest a complimentary ashtray with a Tour d'Argent crest embossed on it. It frequently is the recipient of the ashes from one of my after-dinner cigars.

Our three children had again been excluded from the luncheon. When we left for lunch we were running late, so I handed my eldest son Fritz a handful of francs and pointed him toward a restaurant a short way from the hotel and told him to take his brother and sister with him for a nice lunch. I said we would meet them at our hotel after we got back. When we returned to our hotel, our guilty feeling also returned upon hearing that the restaurant we sent them to was closed and they had nothing to eat. We quickly remedied their hunger by taking them to an upscale café near the Place de l'Opéra. Our guilt lessened, but it has never completely disappeared.

Our favorite restaurant in Chicago is Bruna's, the second oldest Italian restaurant in Chicago, which was founded in 1933. It is situated on the south side in the area that used to be known as Little Italy. With the change of demographics in the city, the Italian population that used to live in the area moved out into the suburbs and the area has become more Hispanic in its population. Bruna's is still operating. It has the atmosphere of a true ethnic restaurant with small, unimpressive furnishings and great food. The last time I was there I had the best veal chop I have ever eaten. While I do not get to Chicago that often, whenever I get there, I go to Bruna's, where I am greeted with friendship by Luciano Silvestri, the proprietor who has personally overseen the restaurant on a daily basis for more than forty years.

I was introduced to the restaurant by Carl Petri, a fishing companion on two trips to the Northeast Territories and a former general surgeon at Porter Hospital in Middlebury. He was raised in a house across the street from the restaurant. His father's barbershop was there. There are still wrought iron benches on the street, where in past years local residents would sit and smoke "Parodi" cigars. As Carl had known Luciano for most of his life, the fact that I was a friend of Carl's made me a friend of Luciano's, and often he would join us at the table as we finished dinner for conversation and a grappa on the house. Patronage consists almost entirely of Chicagoans who know they are having the best Italian food in all of Chicago. It is off the beaten path of tourism, and I have often brought friends and colleagues I was working with to the restaurant. The lawyers who I took there always came away with a feeling that this was really a very special place, and many put it on their list of places to go when they returned to Chicago.

Rule's Restaurant on Maiden Lane is the oldest restaurant in London. It may appear a bit upscale when you arrive as there is a well-dressed doorman on the street who welcomes you inside. The history of the restaurant is that it was tied to an up-country farm that supplied some of its produce and its game.

Joann and I often stop there after a matinee at a nearby theater. The food is always high quality, the service impeccable, and it is always a fun dining experience. Both the food and atmosphere have always made for a special occasion. One of the treats is a dessert cheese course of Britain's famous stilton cheese. It is served by the waiter who brings out a whole wheel of stilton and then, with a spoon, cuts into the center of the round wheel, placing generous portions of cheese on your plate. Accompanying the stilton is a silver dish filled with a variety of biscuits and another silver chalice holding stalks of celery. It is best accompanied by a glass of a good port. This whole ceremony adds special significance to a meal at Rule's.

In the 1960s and early 1970s, the best restaurant, at least the best French restaurant, in Vermont was Café Shelburne located across Route 7 from the Shelburne Museum. It was operated by Andre and Danielle Ducolt, a young French couple, and the menu was something you would expect in Paris rather than in Vermont. The food was always good, and it became our favorite dinner outing.

We became good friends with Andre and Danielle. On one occasion, we took them to dinner in the clubhouse at Saratoga raceway to see harness racing on a night I had a horse racing but was not driving. Once they came to have dinner at our home—a bit daunting, but we fared well.

One evening, after dinner at Café Shelburne, Andre came to our table and told us he had a special treat for us. In Montreal, he had bought a bottle of eau de vie, Poire Williams. He could not serve that on the menu as it was not purchased in the Vermont liquor store, a requirement to sell liquor under Vermont law. However, because we were his guests, he could offer us a drink from his own private stock. We were the double beneficiaries, having both our first experience with Poire Williams and having it as a guest rather than as a paying customer.

He brought the bottle to the table, fresh out of the freezer along with two iced glasses. We were invited to help ourselves. The first taste was a brand-new culinary experience for both Joann and myself. Poire Williams has the bite of a cognac, but as the liquor warms it emits the aroma and taste of a fresh pear. Since then, I discovered that there are other eau de vies, including Framboise Sauvage (wild raspberry) and mirabelle (plum). There is seldom a time when I see eau de vie on the menu that I don't order it. A wonderful way to finish a meal.

On a trip through southern France, Joann and I traveled by train to Monaco. Leaving Nice, the train meanders along the coast of the Mediterranean, sometimes going through tunnels eventually stopping at Monte Carlo. The train tracks, the roadways, and virtually the entire city is located high on the dramatic cliffs that lead down to the Mediterranean. Below is the harbor and marina.

In the center of the city, there is a large circle and the famous casino, which is located to the south between the city and the cliffs. On the west side of that circle is the Hotel de France. Joann and I had heard that the Hotel de

France hosted one of Europe's best restaurants, a three-star Michelin: Alain Ducasse's "Le Louis XV." We decided to take a look to see if we could fit a luncheon there into our budget.

As we started towards the hotel, there was a film crew taking up most of the street and the entire front of the hotel. A Lamborghini drove up, and a well-coiffed woman got out and ambled up the steps to the hotel with film crews following her every move.

They were in the process of making a feature film, and the public was temporarily barred from the front entrance. Our alternative was to enter the hotel from the north side, walk through the lobby, and locate Le Louis XV. We found the restaurant and looked at the posted menu, noticing that just an appetizer of asparagus and morels was going for eighty-five euros. This was beyond our budget.

We continued through the lobby, heading towards the exit on the south side, when we were stopped by an employee of the hotel with the inquiry, "Can I help you?" We told him that we had been looking at Le Louis XV, and he, seeing we were walking away, suggested that we look at Le Grill on the top floor. We took his advice and found there was a glassed-in restaurant looking out over the bay, the marina, and the Mediterranean. The entire south walls were glass.

We asked to see a menu and found it had a fixed price luncheon at seventy-five euros. That was within our budget, and we asked for a table.

We were promptly seated at a table near the windows with a view of seagulls flying down below the restaurant and above the harbor. Much to Joann's surprise, the waiter brought a little upholstered stool that was placed next to her chair. It was for her to put her purse on. When we reviewed the menu, we discovered that the fixed price lunch also included wine. A choice of entrée was a beef tenderloin. We ordered it rare, and it arrived cooked to perfection, accompanied by french fries that were almost shoestring-like in size and crisp and delicious. For dessert, we had a crème brûlée.

The surprise of the luncheon, however, was the wine. When the waiter inquired whether we wanted red or white wine, we expected a carafe of a good, local French wine. He returned shortly with a vintage bottle of a Montrachet red. It was a quality of wine beyond which I had ever ordered in a restaurant, and I expect its list price would be more than the cost of the two entire lunches. We were told this wine had been on the wine list of the restaurant on the first floor, and when the supply got down to a point where it could no longer be maintained on that restaurant's wine list, it was sent upstairs to be served with fix-priced lunches. I think our waiter must have taken a liking to us and picked the best available bottle.

After the meal, we continued to enjoy the view and I had a eau de vie framboise sauvage to accompany a #2 Monte Cruz cigar.

Memorable restaurants do not always have to be Michelin starred. One of Joann's and my favorites is a small restaurant located across the street from the British Museum in London. It goes by the unassuming name "Munchkins." Its claim to fame as far as we are concerned, was that it served wonderful kippers. The kippers never seemed to be the same but always were served on a piece of hot buttered toast and always tasted outstanding. Somehow, on each trip to London, we managed at least once to eat breakfast there, always having kippers. It was part of the basis for my often-repeated statement: "I've never met a herring I didn't like."

Joann and I finished off our first European trip in Denmark with a luncheon in Copenhagen. After finishing our entrée, we decided to order crêpe suzette for dessert. Our waiter was a young apprentice about fifteen years of age. He treated us well, and when we ordered the crepe suzette he was excited. Serving of the crêpe suzette was done from a trolley that was brought to the table and prepared in front of you. The young man was thinking he was going to have the opportunity to show off his ability to make a show of preparing the crêpes and the orange sauce that goes with them.

As soon as the senior waiter saw him moving the trolley to our table, he intervened. He told the young man that he would take over and prepare the crêpes, and the young man appeared almost in tears as he was shuttled to stand aside. The senior waiter knew his job and made a fine presentation, but we would have been much happier to have watched the young man learning and trying his skills. As we left the restaurant, I slipped the young man an additional tip and told him that we were sorry he did not get a chance to prepare the dessert. He looked at us and said, "I could have done it; I know I can do it," and we thanked him again as we left.

CHAPTER 19

Potpourri

Greg Bean, the son of Walter Bean, the owner of Lake Dunmore Hotel, got married. His wife came from a well-to-do family and was a bit stiff and formal in her approach to the world. We had not yet met his wife when we invited them to dinner at our old farmhouse.

Before supper we enjoyed martinis. The farmhouse, with its post and beam structure and clapboard siding, was structured with windows on both sides of the house. In the dining room, you have light coming in from both the back and the front of the house. Dinner consisted of lamb chops. After cutting off the better pieces of meat from the chops, Joann and I picked up the bones and started chewing on the meat attached to them. "Nearer the bone, the sweeter the meat." To liven things up a little bit, we finished the bones and both Joann and I threw them over our shoulder onto the floor in the direction of our dogs lying on the floor near the table. The shocked look on Greg's wife's face—both that we had eaten from the bones with our hands and then threw them over our shoulders onto the floor—caused an expression that clearly indicated that this was not what she expected at a dinner party. Joann quickly blurted, "We always feed our dogs this way." After a short while, we explained that we were just pulling her leg and we picked up the bones. The dogs got fed regular kibble. Things loosened up a lot after that, and we had an enjoyable dinner in a much more relaxed fashion.

Middlebury has been blessed from the 1950s forward with the Middlebury Community Players, a group utilizing local talent who put on several productions yearly. On occasion, to supplement plays and as an annual musical, they would sponsor a traveling group of young professional actors to put on a play. These occasions usually rallied a decent audience—depending on what venue could be obtained for the production. This was long before the current Town Hall Theater was renovated into the modern theater that exists today.

On one occasion, Joann and I attended a play and then decided to go to The Middlebury Inn and visit the Pine Room, its bar, for a nightcap. While we were there, the cast of the visiting company came in to also have a nightcap. We started a conversation, and then they soon found out that while drinks were available, it was too late for food service. The actors had not had supper and were hungry. We solved the problem by inviting them to the farm for a late-evening snack. It turned out to be a very fun evening, and the discussion about theater in general was wide ranging.

The best part of it, however, was the fact that the snack we were able to serve them consisted principally of two things. We had a haunch of roasted venison that still contained a sizable amount of meat that the two of us had not done much damage to in our earlier meal. Also, in the freezer, we had frozen a large number of escargots. The escargots were put into their shells with an ample portion of garlic butter and then frozen. They merely had to be taken from the freezer and heated in the oven and presented as a high-quality gourmet treat.

Joann and I will never forget the company and the joy we had in presenting such an unusual and fun late-evening snack. I am sure it was also a sharing of food that the actors will never forget.

Many out of town visitors to New York City think that the people living there are reserved and humorless. While it may be hard to make eye contact with New Yorkers on the street or on subways, it is by no means an indication that they lack cordiality and a sense of humor, albeit humor of its own kind.

On a trip to New York City to argue a case before the Second Circuit Court of Appeals, I stayed at the Salisbury Hotel in Midtown. I got up early for a walk to a corner on 57th Street, which housed Wolfe's Delicatessen. As my argument was scheduled for 10:00 am, I had time for a relaxing breakfast. The person I believed to be the proprietor greeted me as I came in and directed me to a seat at a table near a window. My leisurely breakfast consisted of one-half of a cantaloupe, a smoked fish plate, a bagel, and coffee. When I finished my breakfast, I took my tab to the cash register and again encountered the same person who had first welcomed me. He took my tab and proffered cash saying, "Your last meal?" I smiled and answered, "If there were half-sour pickles on the table, I would have eaten more." Without a second delay, he hollered to Joe behind the take-out counter: "Give this man a couple of half-sour pickles." Joe wrapped up two half-sours in a piece of aluminum foil and handed it to me with the comment, "You don't look pregnant." It was a moment of pure New York humor. It turned out later that I represented the proprietor's nephew in a transaction involving a chain of restaurants. I related this story to him without knowing I was telling a story about his uncle. He smiled and said, "That's my uncle, that's for sure."

Another example of a New Yorker's sense of humor was on another trip to New York where I was staying in Midtown at the St. Moritz. When I walked into the registration desk, I was behind two gentlemen having a friendly discussion. The desk clerk, who looked like he had started work there during the Coolidge administration, acknowledged them with, "Can I help you?" One of the men turned from his conversation towards the clerk and said, "I have a reservation and I would like a room facing the park." The St. Moritz is on Central Park South; the front of the building has a good view of Central Park looking uptown. The desk clerk, who I am sure had served pompous politicians and celebrities of all sorts, did not take kindly to the rather arrogant assertion by this new customer. He responded, "I'm sorry, sir, we are quite full. We do have a room for you, but I'm afraid it's in the back of the house." The client unhappily signed the registration form, took his key, and went off with his friend. I was next in line and stepped up to the desk: "I don't care where you put me as long as it's got a bed in it." The clerk smiled appreciating that I had heard his handling of the previous customer. "Don't worry, I'll take care of you." I got a large room on the sixteenth floor facing Central Park. Justice prevails.

Once at LaGuardia Airport, I was again second in line at a time of weather complications delaying flights. The person in front of me, stranded by the delay, was taking it out verbally on the ticket agent. The fact that the agent had no control over the weather did not stop the individual from berating her in a most obnoxious fashion. After he left, I asked the agent, "How do you put up with that?" "It's easy. I just sent his baggage to Hamburg, Germany." Justice prevails again?

Vermonters love to have potluck suppers, BBQs, and any excuse for sharing food with their neighbors. In the 1960s, the annual Salisbury Town Meeting still included a potluck luncheon. In part, it was really a competition of who made the best baked beans and the best apple pie. The town meetings, a democratic tradition, harbored discussion of serious town issues, which sometimes turned humorous. Attending my first town meeting in 1961, Harry Sullivan, purported to know more when he was dead drunk than the rest of the men in town did put together sober) started a discussion with the road commissioner. The topic involved the formula for receiving state aid for the town roads. Harry apparently was fully acquainted with the subject and went on for about five minutes, explaining why the town was not following the right procedures. I was sitting in the chair next to him. Not only was I a new lawyer, but I was the only lawyer in the town and attending my first town meeting. When he finished his tirade, he turned to me: "Now isn't that right, Mr. Langrock?" He was looking for the imprimatur of a lawyer on his elaborate dissertation concerning the formula for state aid to town roads and why the road commissioner was wrong. I had no idea what he was talking about. I had two choices: I could either agree or not agree. If I agreed, he had obtained a legal imprimatur for his position. If I disagreed, I was sure he would have taken me on, and I never would have been able to defend my position. I took the easy way out. "Looks right to me, Harry." That ended the discussion just in time for the potluck luncheon. I love baked beans and apple pie, making these meals a treat to me—a treat not only for the food but for the goodwill and companionship of the citizens who turned out for the town meeting.

At one town meeting, a controversy arose concerning a proposed dog leash law for the village. Seeley Reynolds, a town father, supported the ordinance, saying that he was tired of seeing dogs run loose in town and opining that they would get to running deer. "If I see a dog chasing a deer, don't you think I wouldn't shoot it?" At this point, Harvey Drinkwine, a breeder of beagles who lived outside the village, chimed in, "If you shoot one of my beagles, I'll shoot you." The tension in the air was a little thicker than usual. Forest Wimmett, well-liked but not a town father, interjected,

"Just the other day I was out in the woods when I saw a doe come through panting, tongue hanging out with a dog right on its trail. You can bet that I took care of that dog." At this point, I blurted, "Well, Forest, what about the doe?" The tension broke, there was laughter all around, and once again we adjourned to the companionship of the town potluck lunch.

Unfortunately, the Australian ballot has taken over much of the controversial matters at the annual town meeting. The one-on-one discussion that used to deal with town issues is now more of a show-and-tell operation rather than a debating society. As the meetings are now held on a convenient evening rather than on what used to be Town Meeting Day (the second day in March) when most businesses used to close has also led to the demise of the potluck luncheon.

The lunch tradition survives in a different setting by the Addison-Bridport Detective Society at its annual meeting. This is an organization that started in 1816 as a vigilante group to stop horse thieves and other lawbreakers. Its members were paid fifty cents a day to track down rustlers and thieves. Its last case was in 1926 when it offered a reward of fifty dollars in connection with a robbery at the general store at Addison Four-Corners. The members saw someone wearing a pair of new pants, and he finally confessed and served some time in jail on Washington Street in Middlebury, the county seat. The Society now consists of a membership of citizens of Bridport and Addison who are willing to pay one dollar a year in dues. There are a variety of honorary members as well, mostly people who have previously given speeches at the annual meeting. Each year, a talk is given by somebody either of local or state-wide interest, thereby earning the "prestige" of becoming a member of the society.

I gave a talk at one meeting and became a member. I always try to make the annual meeting, which is held just before a lunch consisting of chicken and biscuits and a Jello salad. Of course, the beverage is cold Vermont milk. At these meetings, I renew acquaintances with farmers I have known for many years but rarely have occasion to visit with.

Another tradition of comradery at meals are the various game suppers held by organizations throughout the state. Fish and Game Clubs to Masonic Lodges hold fundraising suppers where wild game seized by wardens or killed on the road consists of servings of venison, occasionally moose, bear, geese, and even occasionally raccoons or beaver. While the food is a draw to these dinners, it is really the companionship of breaking bread with a group of people you know well but see only occasionally that draws the crowds. The stories about missed shots or about the big buck you shot years ago and the mismanagement of the deer herd keeps the conversation lively.

I had a fraternity brother, Robert, who was involved with me in the Canterbury Club, which was the student organization affiliated with the Episcopal Church. The club would often have a Sunday dinner with a meeting beforehand. Robert and I would attend the first part of the meeting and sneak out towards the end. We would make a quick trip up to 57th Street and go to Jimmy's (a bar that is familiar to most students at the University of Chicago) and have a quick martini. We would then get back to the club just in time for dinner. Dinners were much more relaxed for us.

Robert's family had a tradition that I was included in on several occasions. This was a Sunday dinner at mid-day. Before dinner, we were all served whiskey sours from a pitcher. The striking thing about dinner was on each occasion there was a topic for discussion. One time it was about Japanese architecture, and the entire conversation was directed towards this topic. It was always intellectually stimulating as all of the family and guests got actually curious about the topics and shared their knowledge. A wonderful tradition, though unfortunately I have never been in a situation where I could perpetuate it.

Kim and Sue Sparks take their croquet seriously—well, almost seriously. For many years, during the summer months, we had a family competition. Both families had a Jacques croquet set. At least once a week we would play a match alternating weekly from one home to the other. There were certain protocols we observed in the game that were outside the general rules. The most important protocol was that we started the match with very dry Beefeater martinis up with an olive. The croquet field was our front lawn, and as we placed the hoops and the stakes, we also placed a small table for our martinis. Somehow the martinis were finished just as we finished the first half of the match. The additional protocol was to have a second martini to finish off the match.

We had a silver-plated dish (which was an heirloom that was handed down from Joann's mother). It had a raised panel of Pancho Villa jousting at windmills. This became the trophy of the competition. The winner took it home and kept it as long as their winning streak continued. Croquet can be highly competitive and requires coordination between teammates to make sure you or your partner has the last ball standing. No quarter was given and none asked for in the competition. Our matches were always followed by dinner, ending with a brandy and, for Kim and myself, a cigar.

CHAPTER 20

German Heritage

In 1871, my great-grandfather Gustave Langrock immigrated from Leipzig Germany, to Astoria in Queens. His trade was wood working, and he came as a wood carver for Steinway Piano Company. Steinway's headquarters were in Astoria, and each year there would be a Steinway Day Parade. According to my father, his grandfather would lead the parade and my father would march along holding his hand. I never knew my great-grandfather, but some of the stories about him were passed down orally. Two of them involved breaking bread.

There were six children in the family, and each Sunday they gathered for a family dinner. The atmosphere was a bit Prussian with my great-grandmother at one end of the table, the six children seated three on each side of the table, and my great-grandfather at the head of the table. He was a city man through and through, from Leipzig to New York City without ever experiencing the countryside. However, he happened to have a friend who was a hunter who had presented him with a large rabbit. On Sunday, Great-grandmother duly roasted the rabbit—hasenpfeffer—and it was presented as a whole roast at the table. The roasted rabbit appeared with all its four limbs sticking up, looking more like an "enfant roti" or a skinned cat than it did the usual Sunday roast. My great-grandfather had no desire to cut into the rabbit, but his Prussian macho background would not let him back down, and he finally summoned the courage to start. The children were less than enthusiastic about this Sunday dinner. Just as my great-grandfather stuck the fork into the rabbit, holding a carving knife in his other hand, one of the children quietly let out a "meow." My great-grandfather, exercising his concept of discipline, sent all six children to their rooms without dinner and the rabbit to the waste bin. It was a hungry Sunday, but all-in-all everybody was happy to avoid eating the rabbit—saved by the anonymous 'meow.' My great-grandfather was able to save face and still maintain authority.

On another occasion, he purchased fruit from a street vendor. It was the first grapefruit he had ever seen, and he assumed it was a large orange. He called the family together to share a taste of this beautiful fruit. He carefully peeled it, divided it into sections, and, as was his prerogative and his duty, took the first bite. "Oh, so sour," he blurted out with a surprised look on his face. That, too, went into the waste bin. These disasters seemed to carry more weight in re-telling than many of the culinary successes.

One success was that my great-grandmother taught her daughter-in-law how to make sauerbraten. Her recipe has been handed down through my father to me, and as far as I know, the recipe has never been written down. Once or twice a year, I make sauerbraten with kartoffle kloesse and invite friends for a German-style dinner.

Sauerbraten is made by pickling a large piece of beef—usually a round roast—in vinegar, water, and pickling spices for about four days. The roast is then removed from the pickling brine—the brine being saved for the gravy. It is then floured and browned in a pot where it is reunited with the brine and cooked until tender. The meat is good, but the secret of the meal is in the gravy and the kartoffle kloesse. The kartoffle kloesse are made by ricing some peeled boiled potatoes, mixing them with breadcrumbs, and egg and spicing with salt, pepper, and a touch of nutmeg. Small croutons made out of white bread seasoned in butter form the center of the dumplings. Each dumpling is a bit smaller than the size of a baseball. The dumplings are then rolled in flour to help prevent them from disintegrating while cooking. The dumplings are dropped into gently boiling water where they immediately fall to the bottom of the pan, then, after a minute or two, they rise to the top of the water. When they hit that top, they are ready to be served. I always claim that my dumplings are so light I have to catch them as they rise before they hit the ceiling.

The real secret is in the gravy. The mixture of vinegar and water in which the meat is pickled over several days is augmented by raisins that have been soaked in a portion of the brine. This mixture is then thickened by ground-up gingersnaps that combine to make a thick sweet-and-sour gravy with plumped raisins included. It is served by slicing the beef and serving it with the kartoffle kloesse, which are broken open, showing the croutons in the center. Everything is then flooded with gravy. Often sweet-and-sour red cabbage is served with it. The combination of sweet-and-sour flavors is dangerous because they are so good you end up eating more than you probably ought to.

— Conclusion —

I hope you have enjoyed these stories about eating and drinking that have formed so much of my life experiences. While the term "breaking bread" has biblical roots, this is not limited to any particular religion or any religion at all. Once you have sat down with a person and shared food, you have also shared tales that have meaning to each of your lives. There is no need for the experience be limited to high-quality restaurants or bars. A shared hotdog or a glass of beer or a cup of coffee changes your relationship with that person forever. Most times it is a positive change, and both you and your companion will profit from it. Hopefully, the reader, on reflection, will think back over the wonderful times he or she has had in this act of sharing.

In a time when so much social contact is conveyed over cell phones or other electronic media, I hope this book can remind you of the importance of real in-person contact and how food and drink help bring people together. There are no cell phone stories in this book.

As we all have some future ahead of us, it is worthwhile to think of future acts of sharing and the meaningful reactions that will be brought about by it. Enjoy the wonders of sharing of food and drink—whether at home or at a public venue—and share the related stories and live your life to the fullest.

— Acknowledgements —

No book is created without the help of many people. Some reminded me of details of stories, others helped me with the deficiencies I have in modern electronics. I would especially like to call attention to my legal assistant Tina Curler and my family friend Laurie Wilson, who helped with the mechanical aspects of putting this book together. Special thanks to my wife, Joann, who puts up with me in a variety of endeavors. Thank you also to Onion River Press—it has been fun working with you.